SYNTHETIC MATERIALS & THE THEORY OF INTERNATIONAL TRADE

SYNTHETIC MATERIALS AND THE THEORY OF INTERNATIONAL TRADE

by

G. C. HUFBAUER

Department of Economics
University of New Mexico

GERALD DUCKWORTH & CO. LTD
3 Henrietta Street, London, W.C.2

First published 1966

© 1966 by G. C. HUFBAUER

*Printed in Great Britain
by Photolithography
Unwin Brothers Limited
Woking and London*
(3629 L)

CONTENTS

LIST OF TABLES

LIST OF DIAGRAMS

PREFACE

THE genesis of this book was my Cambridge University Ph.D. thesis, *Synthetic Materials: A Study in International Trade*, 1963. Many individuals and institutions generously assisted in its preparation and subsequent revision. It is a pleasure to record the debts which I owe to them. Chemical firms and trade associations throughout the world answered numerous questions. The staff at the London Board of Trade Library helped me gather statistical material. The Marshall Commission kindly granted a three-year scholarship which enabled me to pursue the necessary research at King's College, Cambridge. And the University of New Mexico provided funds for additional statistical work and the final manuscript revision.

Nicholas Kaldor, my thesis supervisor, deserves special thanks for untiring criticism and inspiring suggestions. His counsel immeasurably improved the finished product. M. V. Posner not only supplied the theoretical foundation for this study, but also gave much practical advice on converting it from a thesis into a book. A. Maizels rendered a great deal of valuable assistance on statistical questions. Larry Saiers, A. H. Vanags, and Parker Fowler helped collect and process data. My wife gave continual support and encouragement; she also worked to improve the style and make it more intelligible to non-economists. The faults which remain are my own.

G. C. HUFBAUER

University of New Mexico
January 1966

Chapter I

AN INTRODUCTION

BANANAS are grown in tropical regions, and coal is mined where lush forests once stood. But scientific progress has created a class of industries not dependent upon climate or natural resources for their location. The manufacture of most synthetic materials—plastics, synthetic rubbers, and man-made fibres—belongs to this class. Because of its independence from nature's endowments, the "footloose" synthetic materials industry provides a challenging study in international trade. The purpose of this book is to examine, in the light of economic theory, both the pattern of national location in the synthetic materials industry, and the trade flows emerging from the industry's development.[1]* This study does not, however, evaluate national gains (or losses) arising from synthetic materials trade.

The basis of trade, whether international or interregional, lies in comparative cost differences which are not neutralised by transport costs. Without trade, as Torrens and Ricardo pointed out, the ratios at which goods exchange within one country probably differ from the ratios at which the same goods exchange within another country. Trade thus enables each country to buy some goods abroad more cheaply than at home. If a bushel of wheat exchanges for three yards of cloth in England and for one yard of cloth in America, English merchants can advantageously trade cloth for wheat. The same reasoning applies, even though without trade America manufactures no cloth, provided that Americans are prepared to pay more than one bushel of wheat for three yards of cloth. The comparative cost framework thus embraces both those instances where trading partners produce similar goods before trade, and instances where they produce dissimilar goods.

The goods each nation should import and export can be predicted once comparative cost differences are known. But economists are not content simply to predict trade patterns from a list

* Footnotes of a reference nature are placed at the end of each chapter. Such footnotes are numbered.

of pre-trade prices. They have inquired more deeply into the nature of international trade. Many theories have been constructed to elucidate why, without trade, the same commodities should exchange at different ratios in various countries, and why some goods are peculiar to certain countries. These theories are grouped together as nature-of-trade theories. Three such nature-of-trade theories appear most relevant to the experience of "footloose" industries (such as synthetic materials): the factor proportions account, the scale economy account, and the technological gap account. The first two theories primarily emphasise static conditions *external* to the individual industry, while the third theory focuses on dynamic developments *within* each industry.

Before examining these theories, it should be mentioned that nature's uneven distribution of basic resources does not primarily shape synthetic materials trade. The scarce basic resources important for today's synthetic materials industries are coal, petroleum, natural gas, sulphur, and pulp wood.[2] Of the major synthetic materials exporting nations, the United States alone is well endowed with each resource. Germany, the United Kingdom, and France lack petroleum and sulphur, and their wood tracts and natural gas fields are limited. Japan is poorly endowed except for coal and sulphur, and sulphur is the only resource Italy has long exploited in abundance (she recently discovered extensive natural gas fields).

These observations suggest that the major exporting nations must obtain many essential resources from foreign nations without paying prohibitive transport costs. Otherwise synthetic materials exports would come from areas better endowed with natural resources. And indeed, Europe and Japan obtain all their petroleum and most of their sulphur abroad; Italy, Germany, and the United Kingdom have relied on Sweden, Canada, and South Africa for pulp wood; and even the United States imports large quantities of petroleum and pulp wood. On the other hand, many well-endowed nations have not yet translated their natural resources into synthetic materials exports. The Middle East and Venezuela, despite their petroleum wealth, do not yet produce (much less export) plastics or synthetic rubber,* while a generous supply of pulp wood has not made Canada a major viscose rayon exporter.† It must be concluded— and a more detailed examination of transport costs in Appendix A supports this conclusion—that the location of raw materials has had little impact on the location of synthetic materials production.

The Factor Proportions Account. The most celebrated nature-of-trade theory is the Heckscher–Ohlin factor proportions account.[3] The basic Heckscher–Ohlin framework can be extended to include any number of productive factors; but such extension ordinarily devalues the theory from the level of explanation to the level of description. We shall therefore adhere to the standard two-factor, two-country, two-commodity model. As an explanation of comparative cost differences in "footloose" manufacturing industries, the factor proportions account relies on four central assumptions.[4]

First, the factor proportions account assumes that factors of production do not cross international boundaries, however mobile they are within a country.

Second, it assumes that production functions permit the unambiguous classification of commodities according to factor-intensity regardless of relative factor prices (the "strong factor-intensity hypothesis").

Third, the account assumes that all countries possess equal technology.

---

* Kuwait, at last realizing the opportunities lost, hired an Italian firm to build a petrochemical complex for manufacturing polyvinyl chloride plastic in 1963 (32 years after Germany) and styrene synthetic rubber in 1965 (24 years after America). As the trade journal commented, "Natural gas is abundantly available, in fact it is currently flared, and this is certainly wasteful . . ." *Chemische Industrie International*, December 1962.

† Earlier periods offer similar examples. Celluloid, the first plastic discovered, incorporates large amounts of camphor. Formosa and Japan supplied the bulk of world camphor needs before synthetic camphor was invented. But Formosa has never produced celluloid, and Japan did not commence manufacture until 1908, almost forty years after America. In fact, for a long while camphor was shipped in the crudest state. Yet the additional costs of transporting "dead weight" impurities made very little difference to celluloid manufacturers in Europe and America. The *Oil, Paint, and Drug Reporter* of March 8, 1882, furnishes a bizarre account: "It will surprise no one to know that with a substance so comparatively costly as camphor, adulterations are very common. Stones, sand, but chiefly fine pulverized salt, are frequently found in the masses of crude material . . . It is said that a Boston manufacturer found the head of a negro in a chest of this substance."

Fourth, it assumes constant returns to scale in the production of each commodity.

Diagram 1–1 illustrates the Heckscher–Ohlin theory with capital and labour as factors of production, and synthetic rubber and man-made fibre as commodities.[5] The heavy convex lines show production functions for arbitrary but equal quantities of rubber and fibre. Since technology, by the third assumption, is the same in Britain and America, the same production functions apply to both countries. Clearly rubber production is always more capital-intensive than fibre production, regardless of relative factor prices.* Moreover, the assumption of constant returns to scale ensures that for any other arbitrary amounts of the two commodities, rubber would still prove more capital-intensive than fibre. For when technology is characterised by constant returns to scale, a single production isoquant (as those in Diagram 1–1) fully defines the shape of the production function for all output quantities.

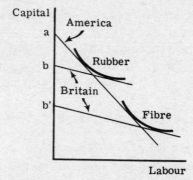

Diagram 1–1.   Theoretical Exposition (Factor Proportions Theory)

The light lines in Diagram 1–1 show American and British factor price ratios. Capital per man is larger in America than in Britain, and consequently wages are higher relative to profits in America. This fact is portrayed by the slopes of the factor price ratio lines, although Diagram 1–1 does not explicitly indicate capital and labour quantities. Since the factor price ratio lines are tangent to the production functions, they indicate the lowest

* Throughout this study, "capital-intensive" and "labour-intensive" refer to capital: labour ratios.

cost of producing rubber and fibre in each country. In the United States, the cost of producing a kilogram of either rubber or fibre is the same. The intersection of the American factor price ratio line with the capital axis at point *a* shows this cost. But in Britain, a single factor price ratio line is not tangent to both production functions. Therefore, a kilogram of British rubber is dearer than a kilogram of British fibre, as shown by the different intersection points of the two factor price ratio lines with the capital axis (*b* and *b'* respectively). Since synthetic rubber and man-made fibre exchange at different ratios in the two countries, the requisite comparative cost differences for trade have been established.

But the Heckscher–Ohlin account goes beyond the mere establishment of comparative cost differences. It asserts that each country exports that commodity which is most intensive in the country's abundant factor. Britain exports labour-intensive man-made fibre, and American exports capital-intensive man-made rubber. This result largely follows from the supposition that technology is everywhere the same; but it also depends, as we shall see, on constant returns to scale and the strong factor-intensity hypothesis. Let us now examine these assumptions, which underlie the factor proportions account.

The first assumption prevented factors of production from migrating across international borders. This assumption preserves factor endowment differences once trade has opened, and thus preserves the basis for factor proportions trade. Although factors do sometimes move from one country to another, the very great differences in living standards between rich and poor nations testify to the general immobility of capital and labour. We need not, therefore, quarrel with factor immobility as an approximate description of modern conditions.

The second assumption stipulated that commodities can be unambiguously classified according to factor-intensity. The "strong factor-intensity hypothesis", as this assumption is sometimes called, has been empirically challenged by at least one writer.[6] But while factor-intensity "reversals"* may occasionally characterise the

---

* A reversal occurs when, for example, paper products are labour-intensive in Japan *vis-à-vis* textiles, but capital-intensive in America *vis-à-vis* textiles.

international economy, their widespread presence has yet to be shown. In the early 1950s, the ordering of American industries by capital-intensity was quite similar to the ordering of Japanese industries by capital-intensity. Since the United States and Japan represent extreme factor price ratio positions, the similarity between the two countries offers much support for the strong factor-intensity hypothesis. Likewise, the ordering of industries in Britain and America was extremely similar during the early 1930s. The factor-intensity reversal question receives further discussion in Appendix B. Based on the arguments presented there, we shall accept the assumption that commodities can be unambiguously classified according to factor-intensity.

The third assumption underlying the factor proportions doctrine stipulated that technology is the same in all countries. This assumption may be examined by considering two mutually exclusive cases. In the first case, factor-substitution is ruled out. Thus, capital and labour must always be combined in the same proportion to produce "output". In the second case, factor substitution is permitted.

If factor substitution is impossible, and technology is the same everywhere, output per man-year must also be the same everywhere. For in every country, a man works with the same quantity of capital and enjoys access to the same know-how. Accordingly, to the extent that wages per man-year are lower in one country than another, profits per man-year must be higher. Broadly speaking, the two components of income—wages and profits—constitute the sum-total of a man-year's output in manufacturing endeavour, and this total must be everywhere identical. Let us now examine the proposition that the sum of wages and profits per man-year is the same in all nations, using America and Japan as illustrative countries.

American 1960 wages per man-year were about $5,000, and Japanese 1960 wages were less than $1,000.[7] As a rule, profits claim at least 25% of American national income. American profits per man-year were thus about $1,667 in 1960. Therefore, presuming that both countries do use the same technology and that factor substitution is impossible, 1960 Japanese profits would have had to be $5,667 to satisfy the third assumption of the factor proportions account. For by this assumption,

(1) American wages per man-year+American profits per man-year of output=Japanese wages per man-year+ Japanese profits per man-year of output;

or,

(2) $5,000+$1,667=$1,000+$5,667.

In short, the absolute difference in profits per man-year of output between the two countries would have had to be as great as the absolute difference in wages per man-year. Put another way, profits would have had to claim 85% of Japanese national income ($5,667/$6,667=85%). This is clearly absurd.

If factor substitution is permitted, both countries will not use the same technique in producing "output". Instead, Japan will employ a more labour-intensive technique than America. Thus, in Diagram 1–2, Japan uses technique *j* while America uses

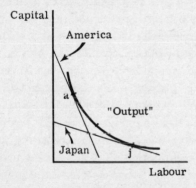

Diagram 1–2. Theoretical Exposition (Factor Proportions Theory)

technique *a*. As a result, Japanese output per man-year is smaller than American output per man-year, even though both countries employ the same production function. When output per man-year differs solely because of capital-intensity variations, the condition that profit differences must be as large as wage differences for empirical experience to satisfy the third assumption of the factor proportions account requires restatement.

Japan uses a more labour-intensive technique and hence, according to the factor proportions theory, has lower output per worker. But since it is open to Japan (under the hypothesis of identical production functions) to produce "output" with the *same* technique as America (technique *a*), a more labour-intensive technique will be used in preference to America's capital-intensive technique only if it yields a higher rate of profit than the American technique would have yielded. Inasmuch as Japan could have earned an 85% profit *share* of output by using the American technique (see the above calculations), she will use a more labour-intensive technique only if the profit share of output is greater *after allowing for the difference in capital : output* ratios. Thus, suppose that the labour-intensive technique involves a capital : output ratio of 2 : 1, whereas the American technique involves a capital : output ratio of 4 : 1. If Japan employs the labour-intensive technique, then the share of profits in output must exceed 42½% to be consistent with the proposition that technology is the same everywhere.

But even during the buoyant post World War II period, the Japanese share of profits in output has normally been less than 35%. Japanese capital : output ratios must thus be less than half those prevailing in the United States—if we are to accept the assumption of equal technology. In the synthetic materials industries, however, capital : output ratios do not usually vary extensively between countries on account of true factor substitution. Nor is there evidence that capital : output ratios in the industrial sector as a whole vary as widely between countries as observed wage and profit differences would require in order to be consistent with the suppositions of the factor proportions theory. Hence, even allowing for the possibility of factor substitution, the third assumption of this theory demands extreme credulity.

The catch is not hard to find. Japan produces much less output, for a given quantum of capital and labour, than America. Japan obviously has a less efficient production function than America. Economists of all schools now agree that substantial technological differences do exist between countries.[8] And these differences greatly weaken the factor proportions theory as an explanation of trade. For if international technological disparities are acknowledged, then relative factor prices assume secondary importance in determining trade patterns. In discussing the technological gap account, we shall explore this aspect further.

The fourth assumption underlying the factor proportions

account stipulated constant returns to scale. The primary function of this assumption is to place all producers on an equal footing regardless of the size of their home markets. Factor price ratio differences thus remain the arbiter of comparative advantage (if the assumption of equal technology also holds). However, since pronounced static scale economies characterise the synthetic materials industries, the fourth assumption is not valid for our study.[9]

This concludes our preliminary examination of the factor proportions theory. Considering the weak empirical evidence for the assumptions of equal technology and constant returns to scale, the theory is not promising as an explanation of synthetic materials trade. Chapter 3 nevertheless examines the factor proportions account in greater detail, using evidence on probable international wage and profit differences.

The Scale Economy Account. There are two kinds of scale economies: static and dynamic. Static scale economies require no essential changes in production processes. They are directly obvious to all producers. Static scale economies are thus the familiar scale economies of economic theory.[10] Dynamic scale economies, on the other hand, are economies achieved *as a result* of production experience. Arrow cites an interesting example:[11]

> It was early observed by aeronautical engineers, particularly T. P. Wright, that the number of labor-hours expended in the production of an airframe (airplane body without engines) is a decreasing function of the total number of airframes of the same type previously produced.

It should be obvious that dynamic scale economies in the international context are no more than an explanation, or rationalisation, of international technological disparities. More particularly, to the extent that dynamic scale economies explain these disparities, the country with large past production enjoys superior technology. As Posner has said,[12]

(1) Technology $= f$ (total past production volume).

If either dynamic or static scale economies characterise production, then the groundwork is laid for the scale economy account.

The simplest version of this account assumes that both countries possess the same production circumstances: identical labour force, capital stock, natural resources, and *ability to improve* technology. Trade is then generated by different consumption preferences. Diagram 1–3 illustrates this model. The production possibility frontier, which is the same for both countries, exhibits a convex shape since the sacrifice of each extra ton of man-made fibre yields resources which can produce larger and larger amounts of plastic, and vice versa. The existence of both kinds of scale economies in each industry makes this so. But insofar as the convexity results from dynamic scale economies, the production possibility frontier takes into account *different* technologies. It is therefore not comparable with textbook production possibility frontiers which assume identical technology throughout.[13]

The light lines in Diagram 1–3 indicate American and British consumption indifference curves. At any given exchange ratio between man-made fibre and plastic, Americans prefer plastic while Britons prefer man-made fibre. The tangents of the respective consumption indifference curves to the common production frontier indicate the ratios at which plastic and man-made fibre exchange within the two countries before trade. Since these ratios differ, a comparative cost basis for trade clearly exists. Each country exports its preferred commodity, because, with economies of scale, each country manufactures its preferred commodity most cheaply.

But in the real world, consumption preferences are not the most important influence governing national exploitation of scale economies. Population and per capita income differences exercise a far greater bearing on the size of home markets than do variations in national consumption preferences. Hence the scale economy account essentially asserts that the country with the largest home market—whether the result of population, income, or consumption preference differences—tends to specialise in those commodities which exhibit the *greatest* scale economies.[14] If doubling factor inputs triples man-made fibre output but quadruples plastic output, then America, with her larger home market, will export plastic and Britain will export man-made fibre. *Scale economy trade may therefore be defined as commerce which arises from*

economies of scale—static or dynamic—which are harvested to a different
extent by each nation owing to variations in home market size.

An important "hidden" assumption underlies our exposition of
the scale economy account. It is the assumption that internal commodity price ratios are established in all countries before trade
opens; that is to say, all goods are produced everywhere before
trade commences. Without this assumption we cannot be sure that
the country with the largest home market will produce most
cheaply, and hence export, the commodity which exhibits the
greatest scale economies.* But contrary to this assumption production and trade are normally simultaneous rather than sequential events, at least among manufactured goods.

Nevertheless, there is a circumstance of the real world which
serves much the same function as our hidden assumption. That
circumstance is artificial trade barriers: tariffs and quotas.[15] When
all home markets are partially protected against foreign commodities, the large country enjoys an advantage in the production
of scale economy goods. A small country may first manufacture the
good, and may erect quite a big factory, but tariff barriers tend to
ensure that the large country eventually reaps greater scale economies. The scale economy account therefore turns on artificial trade
barriers, rather than operating in the context of free and costless
exchange of goods. Chapter 4 will explore the theory as an
explanation of synthetic materials commerce in light of this and
other qualifications.

The Technological Gap Account. The last nature-of-trade theory
under examination is the technological gap account. This theory
emphasises dynamic developments within an industry, and thus
seems peculiarly suited to the rapidly growing synthetic materials
industry. Various writers have hinted at the technological gap
account, but its essential elements were explicitly formulated by
M. V. Posner.[16]

Posner first assumes that there are no international differences
in factor endowment proportions and that absolute as well as
relative factor price equality prevails between countries.[17] (After

* If this assumption does not hold, a small country may, for example, erect a large
plant *with a view* to exporting most of the output. In other words, the small country
need not be confined to the horizons of its home market.

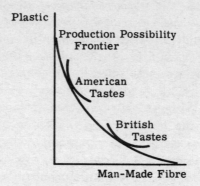

Diagram 1–3. Theoretical Exposition (Scale Economy Theory)

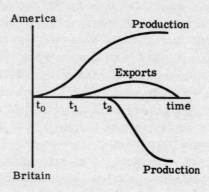

Diagram 1–4. Theoretical Exposition (Technological Gap Theory)

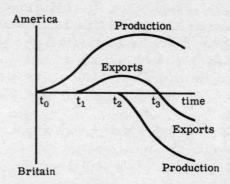

Diagram 1–5. Theoretical Exposition (Technological Gap Theory)

setting forth the basic model, we shall modify this assumption.)
At the outset the two industries, let us say plastics and man-made
fibres, produce identical commodities on both sides of the Atlantic.
Trade is possible, but the British and American economies are so
similar, by virtue of the assumption of equal factor endowments,
that no trade occurs.

Posner then supposes that one country discovers a new product
which it subsequently exports to another country. The new
product competes to some extent with existing goods in both
countries. We may imagine, for example, that an American firm,
Pu Dont, discovers nylon, a remarkable new fibre. Immediately
when nylon becomes available, American textile mills begin
weaving nylon fabrics. Point t_0 marks this event in Diagram 1–4.
(Diagrams 1–4 and 1–5 measure time on the horizontal axis and
production and export quantities on the vertical axis.) Pu Dont
salesmen then approach British textile mills. The British mills
shortly begin placing orders, which leads to American exports of
nylon. The period between initial American nylon consumption
and initial British nylon consumption is called the "demand lag".
Diagram 1–4 shows the demand lag as the distance between t_0
and t_1.

Meanwhile, British rayon producers apprehend the danger to
their markets. Pu Dont's patents securely cover all nylon variations, but Pu Dont eventually grants an exclusive licence to British
Fibres Ltd. British Fibres constructs its own plant, and British
nylon production begins at point t_2. The period between first
American nylon production and first British nylon production,
that is, the distance from t_0 to t_2, is called the "imitation lag". In
this example, licensing is the "imitation route".

Presumably some marginal consideration, such as delivery
schedules, gives each firm an advantage in serving its own home
market. Thus, British Fibres supplies a larger and larger fraction
of the British nylon market, until American nylon exports eventually cease. But while they lasted, American nylon exports were
technological gap trade. For they originated solely in the temporary technological superiority of the American man-made fibre
industry, as reflected in its initial discovery of nylon fibre.

Posner views the total volume of American nylon exports as a function of the difference between demand lag and imitation lag. The longer this difference, the larger will be American exports. Such a relationship seems plausible if the innovating firm (Pu Dont) and the imitating firm (British Fibres) are both important producers relative to firms which later enter the market.

Moreover, Posner has suggested that scale economies, whether static or dynamic, may serve to enlarge technological gap trade. Let us first consider static scale economies. When production and trade are simultaneous events, and when no tariffs or quotas protect home markets, the country with the largest home market need not necessarily reap the greatest scale economies.[18] Instead the innovating country, whether large or small, may build an extensive plant, harvest static scale economies, and prolong its technological gap exports. For an innovating firm enjoys a peculiar advantage in harvesting scale economies. This advantage arises because markets for most new products, including synthetic materials, expand rapidly at first. The innovator can thus more confidently erect large plants and secure an entrenched position in domestic and export markets than can successor firms at home or abroad. Indeed, the innovator may build ahead of home demand specifically to reap scale economies in plant construction, and then view exports as a suitable, if temporary, "vent for surplus".

In other words, the technological gap account presents an alternative to the theory advanced by the scale economy account regarding the exploitation of static scale economies. According to the technological gap theory, a small country which innovates may yet build a large plant; but the scale economy account simply asserts that the country with the greatest home market builds the largest plant, regardless of when it begins production. To the extent that the technological gap theory is correct, static scale economies enhance the volume and prolong the life of technological gap exports. For example, Pu Dont's lead in exploiting static scale economies may sustain American nylon exports even after British Fibres has erected a plant adequate for the British market.

Similarly, temporal differences in undertaking production may condition the exploitation of dynamic scale economies more than pre-existing differences in home market size. The innovating country may, solely as a result of larger accumulated production volume, improve its technology ahead of other nations. For as Posner and Arrow have suggested,[19]

(1) Technology$=f$ (total past production volume).

An innovation may provide a greater stimulus to large accumulated production volume than a big home market, especially since the innovator has a free option on export markets.[20]

However, in the absence of precise information of the origins of technological progress, we shall advance a rather different hypothesis about dynamic scale economies than the Posner–Arrow argument. We shall follow Kaldor in supposing that the *length of time* a country has produced a certain plastic or man-made fibre better reflects its level of technology than the *accumulated volume* of production. To paraphrase Kaldor:[21] "Learning" takes time, as well as activity. Hence the productivity of the nth "machine" will depend not only on the cumulative total of "machines" which have been previously built but on the time interval over which that total was constructed. The higher the rate of production of "machines", and thus the shorter the time interval, the smaller will be the improvement in productivity. Thus,

(2) Technology$=f$ (length of time in production).

This hypothesis about dynamic scale economies makes international technological differences a direct function of the imitation lag in contrast to the indirect and less certain relationship which the Posner–Arrow argument suggests. If Switzerland has produced epoxy resins ten years and Germany only two years, then according to the Kaldorian hypothesis Swiss technology ought to be superior, even though German accumulated production volume is larger.

If this hypothesis is correct, then dynamic scale economies behave very much like static scale economies in enhancing the volume of technological gap trade. For example, by the time British Fibres starts nylon production, Pu Dont may have considerably improved its own nylon technology. And even if it wishes to do so, Pu Dont may not be able to communicate the entire body of its know-how to British Fibres. A large part of technology inevitably consists of labour's familiarity with the product and process at hand, and oftentimes this familiarity cannot be easily communicated to a foreign country. Pu Dont may therefore prolong the life of her technological gap exports by cutting costs one step ahead of British Fibres, even though British Fibres erects a plant as large as its American counterpart (and hence as economical from the static scale economy viewpoint). But eventually improvements in nylon technology will be exhausted. British Fibres can then catch up, technologically, with Pu Dont, and American nylon exports will finally cease.

There are two legitimate criticisms to our dynamic scale hypothesis. First, differences in initial production dates for very old products may have little bearing on present day technological disparities. Although Britain began manufacturing celluloid plastic in 1877, seven years after America, this meant practically nothing in 1960, inasmuch as celluloid technology had long since been perfected in both countries. The second criticism is that initial production dates and imitation lags only refer to the first producing firm in each country. Other firms are simply ignored. Thus, even though our hypothesis might be sound when applied to a single firm, extending it to a whole country may introduce distortions.

The first criticism clearly calls for some weighting procedure whereby the importance of the imitation lag in measuring technological disparities diminishes as the product grows older. Unfortunately no empirical basis exists for devising such a procedure. Without being purely arbitrary, it is impossible to accommodate this criticism. For we have no way of knowing whether a ten-year lag incurred in undertaking the manufacture of a product which was first introduced a century ago has one-twentieth, one-tenth, or one-quarter the importance of a ten-year lag incurred in a product first introduced fifteen years ago. However, if in adding together imitation lags for various products, the imitation lag for each product is weighted by the output of that product, the resulting *aggregate* imitation lag will in fact minimise the role of older products.[22] This is true because newer products normally far outsell their predecessors. And since our statistical analysis deals entirely in aggregate imitation lags, this method of weighting individual lags may partially answer the first criticism.

The second criticism in effect demands a much more ambitious study than we could undertake. To answer this criticism it would be necessary to gather first production dates from *all* firms in each country, and then devise some method of weighting the various dates. Such a project was beyond our resources. Furthermore, there are good rationalisations for letting the experience of the first producing firm represent the experience of the whole industry in a given country. Normally the first producing firm in each country stands among the most important firms. Its own experience, therefore, in large part determines overall industry efficiency. Moreover, since the mobility of highly-skilled labour is much greater between firms of the same nationality than between firms of contrary nationalities, technology is usually much more homogeneous within a country than between countries. For these reasons, the imitation lag should furnish a rough guide to national technological differences.

The foregoing discussion of technological gap trade, and its relation to static and dynamic scale economies, enables a more precise definition of this type of commerce than hitherto given. It was assumed, let us recall, that both countries have identical factor endowment proportions and factor price ratios. Hence, aside from temporary differences in technology, no comparative cost basis for trade exists. *Technological gap trade is therefore the impermanent commerce which initially arises from the exporting nation's industrial breakthrough, and which is prolonged by static and dynamic scale economies flowing from that breakthrough.*

We should now modify the assumption which stipulated equal factor endowment proportions and equal factor prices between countries.[23] Contrary to this assumption, major factor endowment and factor price differences do exist. What effect do these differences exert upon the technological gap account?

The key to this question lies in the source of factor price ratio differences. These differences primarily stem not from variations in the division of the economic pie (as the factor proportions theory would assert), but from substantial changes in the size of the pie itself. That is to say, the American wage:profit ratio greatly exceeds the Japanese wage:profit ratio, not because profits are much larger in Japan, but because wages are much smaller.[24] Wages reflect productivity, and international productivity disparities can ordinarily be traced to longstanding differences in the application of science to industrial problems.* As a general rule, countries with low wages are therefore not technological leaders. Naturally there are exceptions: for example, Japan has pioneered in the development of polyvinyl alcohol fibres. But the general rule may be adopted as a working hypothesis.

Given the general rule, it follows that technological gap exports do not normally originate in low-wage countries. Such exports depend upon scientific and industrial leadership: discovering, developing, and marketing the new product ahead of other countries. And this leadership is not typical of low-wage countries. Instead, technological gap exports are usually characteristic of high-wage countries.

But less developed nations can lay claim to another species of industrial export: low-wage trade. *By low-wage trade, we mean exports from low-wage countries to high-wage countries which are predicated on lower wage costs*. Since high profit rates seldom compensate altogether for low wage rates, it might at first appear that low-wage trade could occur in any commodity. For very few industrial commodities are sufficiently capital-intensive that, merely on the basis of international differences in profit rates, the high-wage country is guaranteed a comparative advantage. However, the comparative advantage of the high-wage country normally stems not from factor price ratio relationships, but from her technological lead. Thus although low wage exports *could* occur in almost any commodity, they are ordinarily constrained to *older* industrial products. Therein lies the connection between technological gap trade and low-wage trade. Let us illustrate by extending our earlier Anglo-American nylon model.

Relative to America, Britain is a low-wage country. This is so mainly because of overall American technological superiority. As before, Pu Dont, a United States firm, discovers and introduces

---

* Capital endowment per worker is of course higher in high-wage countries. But capital, unlike iron ore or oil, is not a gift of nature. Therefore in offering a broad explanation of productivity differences we must not rest with the simple assertion that capital endowment differs.

nylon. This event is shown by point t_0 in Diagram 1–5. When British Fibres Ltd. acquires the Pu Dont licence for the United Kingdom, the same trade pattern initially transpires as portrayed in Diagram 1–4: British Fibres supplies a larger and larger share of the British market while American exports dwindle. But this time British Fibres need not altogether catch up with Pu Dont's technology, nor build quite as large a plant, in order to terminate American nylon exports. For British Fibres enjoys the compensating advantage of lower wage rates. Hence American technological gap exports may enjoy a shorter life than if the two countries had the same factor costs.[25] Moreover, British Fibres may eventually export nylon on the basis of her lower wage rates. In Diagram 1–5, t_3 marks the point where Britain reverses the trade flow and begins exporting nylon to America. At this point low-wage trade supplants technological gap trade. British low wage nylon exports should continue either until nylon is superseded by another man-made fibre, or until British wage rates rise to the American level.

The full technological gap account thus consists of the temporal sequence of technological gap trade followed by low wage trade. And since we have assumed that high-wage countries normally furnish the leadership in discovering new products, it follows that technological gap trade and low-wage trade will ordinarily flow in *opposite* directions, rather than emanating from the same country.

There are two commonly found variations to the above illustration of the technological gap account.[26] First, technological gap trade may take place between countries, such as Britain and Germany, which are really quite similar with respect to factor endowments and factor prices. In that case, the importing country can never hope to supplant technological gap imports with low wage exports. But she might well develop a new product or variation of her own, and thus exchange technological gap exports for technological gap imports.

Second, when more than two countries are involved, any given country may send technological gap exports to one destination and low-wage exports to another. Suppose in our example that Spain started manufacturing nylon after Britain. Then Britain might send technological gap exports to Spain and low-wage exports to America. The technological gap account thus implies a "pecking order" of trade. The country with the longest imitation lags must rely almost entirely upon low-wage exports to pay for technological gap imports. The country which innovates can largely depend upon technological gap exports to pay for low-wage imports. Between the two extremes, the nation's reliance upon low-wage exports and technological gap imports increases as its imitation lags lengthen.

One element of the technological gap account has been passed over rather hastily: the incentives which spread the manufacture of new products from one nation to another. There are two principal "spreading mechanisms". One spreading mechanism, suggested by Posner, springs from the threat which new products pose to existing goods. Clearly, the more developed a nation's industrial structure, and thus the higher its wage rate, the more likely it is that some firm will view the import of each new synthetic material as a direct peril. For example, American nylon exports to Britain directly challenge the British viscose rayon industry; but American nylon exports to Egypt do not challenge any particular firm or industry. The second spreading mechanism stems from the lure of high profits. The chemical industry typically spreads the manufacture of new synthetic materials, even though its products are less threatened than the products of other industries. The reason for this is that the chemical industry—through familiarity with analogous products and processes—can better evaluate and realise the potential profits of manufacture. Presumably the more developed the chemical industry, the better it can assess profits and overcome difficulties presented by new synthetics. And, of course, a well developed chemical industry normally characterises a high-wage nation. The two spreading mechanisms therefore usually ensure that high-wage countries imitate more rapidly than low-wage countries.

Diagram 1–6 portrays the basic version of the technological gap account for trade between two countries. This diagram shows three sequential stages through which trade passes as the product becomes older. In Stage 1, high-wage Country A sends technological gap exports to low-wage Country B. The threat which these exports pose to certain firms in Country B, and the high

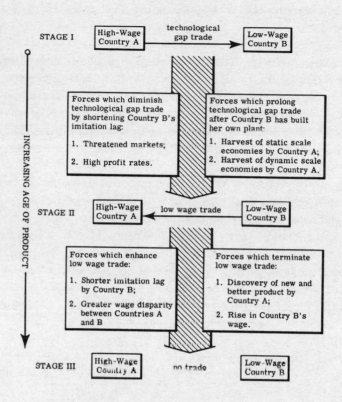

Diagram 1–6. The Technological Gap Account

profits earned by the new product, both induce Country B to erect her own plant. But Country A's lead in exploiting static and dynamic scale economies prolongs her technological gap exports even after Country B has established production facilities at home. Eventually Country B, assisted by lower wage rates, overcomes these disadvantages. In Stage II, Country B's technological gap imports cease, and she begins sending low-wage exports to Country A. Country B's low wage exports are enhanced according as her imitation lag is shorter and her wage disparity with Country A is greater. Sooner or later, however, Country B's low-wage exports dwindle as two other forces take their toll. First, Country B's wages may rise; second, and far more likely, Country A may develop a new product which supersedes the old one thus starting the cycle over again. In Stage III there is no trade.

Forthcoming Chapters. Chapter 2 outlines the salient characteristics of the synthetic materials industry. The historical presentation in this chapter emphasises the sequential entry of producing nations and the development of new markets. Static and dynamic scale economies are explored at length. The chapter concludes with a discussion of the price and profit behaviour encountered in the industry.

Chapter 3 examines the factor proportions theory in light of capital-intensities, and wage and profit rates. Chapter 4 deals with the scale economy theory in a similar vein.

Chapter 5 then turns to an exposition of the imitation lag, thereby setting the stage for the technological gap account. Chapter 6 draws together the various strands of evidence which support Posner's theory.

Chapter 7 summarises the results of our study.

REFERENCES

1. The theoretical exposition primarily draws upon: S. E. Harris, *International and Interregional Economics*, 1957; E. Hoffmeyer, *Dollar Shortage*, 1958; C. P. Kindleberger, *International Economics*, 1963; G. D. A. MacDougall, "British and American Exports: A Study Suggested by the Theory of Comparative Costs; Part I; Part II". *Economic Journal*, December 1951; September 1952; J. E. Meade, *Trade and Welfare*, 1955; S. Mookerjee, *Factor Endowments and International Trade*, 1958; M. V. Posner, "International Trade and Technical Change", *Oxford Economic Papers*, October 1961.

2. Other important, but virtually ubiquitous, basic resources are limestone, water, salt, and air.

3. E. F. Heckscher, "The Effect of Foreign Trade on the Distribution of Income", reprinted in *Readings in the Theory of International Trade*, 1949; B. Ohlin, *Interregional and International Trade*, 1933. A modern restatement of the Heckscher–Ohlin theory is presented by Mookerjee, *op. cit.*

4. Other assumptions, such as perfect competition and internal factor mobility, facilitate the discussion of gains-from-trade, but our study neglects that aspect of commerce.

5. Synthetic materials do, of course, embody other factors, such as water, limestone, coal and oil. However, these quasi-land factors are either ubiquitous or mobile across international borders. In either case, as we have already argued, they do not significantly affect the international location of synthetic materials industries.

6. B. S. Minhas, "The Homohypallagic Production Function", *Journal of Political Economy*, April 1962.

7. The figures are taken from U.S. Department of Commerce, *Statistical Abstract of the United States*, 1962; and International Labour Organisation, *Yearbook of Labour Statistics*, 1961.

8. Recently the neo-classical school has recognised the existence of these differences. See K. J. Arrow, H. B. Chenery, B. S. Minhas, and R. M. Solow, "Capital-Labor Substitution and Economic Efficiency", *Review of Economics and Statistics*, August 1961.

9. See below and Chapter 4.

10. Chapter 2 discusses the type of static scale economies found in the synthetic materials industry. But it is interesting to note here that non-homogeneous scale economies, such as characterise this industry, may lead to factor-intensity reversals. Suppose that output S of synthetic rubber requires \$1 million capital multiplied by 2^y and 100 men multiplied by 2^z. Both y and z are less than one, implying scale economies in both capital and labour usage, but they have different values. The production function is therefore non-homogeneous. As a result, the degree of capital-intensity varies as the scale of output changes. Thus

the synthetic rubber industry might be less capital-intensive than Industry X in a small country, but more capital-intensive than Industry X in a large country. Nevertheless, under these circumstances a factor-intensity reversal has only minor significance. For once scale economies are admitted (non-homogeneous or otherwise) factor-intensity itself assumes a secondary role in determining trade patterns. More important is the extent of scale economies in various industries.

11. K. J. Arrow, "The Economic Implications of Learning by Doing", *Review of Economic Studies*, July 1962, p. 156.

12. M. V. Posner, *op. cit.* In discussing the technological gap account, below, we shall introduce a different version of the dynamic scale economy argument. Chapter 2 outlines the evidence for dynamic scale economies.

13. Compare, for example, P. A. Samuelson, *Principles of Economics*, 1961, Chapter 2. Moreover, the production possibility frontier in Diagram 1–3 is irreversible insofar as it results from the existence of dynamic scale economies, since it only describes the outcome of increasing specialisation in the production of either commodity. Once superior technology has been acquired, it is not likely to be forgotten simply because the country turns to production of the other commodity.

14. Once per capita income differences are admitted as an influence upon market size, factor price ratio differences necessarily exist. And since the scale economy account concentrates on market size rather than factor prices, it must contend with those theories which do consider wage:profit ratios.

15. As the discussion of transport costs indicated, natural trade barriers are unimportant among synthetic materials.

16. M. V. Posner, *op. cit.* Among the economists who have hinted at this theory are C. P. Kindleberger, *op. cit.*, Chapter 7; I. B. Kravis, " 'Availability' and Other Influences on the Commodity Composition of Trade", *Journal of Political Economy*, April 1956; E. Hoffmeyer, *op. cit.*, Chapters 5–7; S. Mookerjee, *op. cit.*, p. 93; and R. Robinson, "Factor Proportions and Comparative Advantage. Part I; Part II", *Quarterly Journal of Economics*, May 1956; August 1956.

17. In addition there are the usual assumptions: no transport costs, international factor immobility, and similar consumer tastes in both countries.

18. Compare our earlier discussion of the scale economy theory.

19. M. V. Posner, *op. cit.*; K. J. Arrow, *op. cit.*

20. In Appendix C we examine this proposed connection between innovation and large accumulated production volume.

21. N. Kaldor, "Comment", *Review of Economic Studies*, July 1962, p. 246.

22. In Chapter 5 the formulation of aggregate imitation lags will be described at greater length.

23. See above, p. 23.

24. Compare the discussion of the assumption of equal technology, pp. 18–20. This matter is considered at greater length in Chapter 3. B. S. Minhas has pointed out that in the early 1950s, profit rates were found to "range from 22 to 15 per cent per annum" while wage rates extended from $250 per annum in the impoverished Asian countries to $3,600 per annum in North America. B. S. Minhas, "The Homohypallagic Production Function", *Journal of Political Economy*, April 1962, p. 146.

25. This statement ignores the general rule that the smaller the wage disparity between the two countries, the shorter will be the imitation lag of the copying nation: see p. 32 below.

26. As a third variation, innovation might take the form of a drastically new process for manufacturing an existing product, rather than the discovery of a new product. But with synthetic materials, the new product is the most significant "unit" of innovation, and process improvement largely comes under the heading of dynamic scale economies.

Chapter 2

CHARACTERISTICS OF THE INDUSTRY

THE synthetic materials industry comprises nearly sixty products.[1] But it ordinarily suffices to speak of just three sub-industries: plastics, synthetic rubbers, and man-made fibres. The present chapter describes the history and structure of these sub-industries, their scale economies, and their pricing behaviour. This short survey obviously cannot document all aspects of synthetic materials. Rather, the descriptive matter has been selected with an eye toward international commerce. In particular, those aspects most relevant to the scale economy theory and the technological gap theory are emphasised. Scale economies, for example, play a vital role in both theories. Accordingly they are described at some length. Likewise, the discussion of industry history revolves around innovation, since innovation occupies a crucial place in the technological gap account. The description of pricing behaviour similarly pays special attention to the international effects of profit patterns.

The pages that follow concentrate upon qualitative rather than quantitative features. Most of the pertinent statistical data has been put in appendices at the end of the book. However, neither the descriptive matter nor the statistical data encompasses the Communist nations, since the nature-of-trade theories under examination clearly may not apply to centralised economies.

History and Structure. The plastics industry was founded with the American manufacture of celluloid in 1870.[2] Celluloid replaced ivory, hard rubber, and horn, largely in luxury and decorative outlets. It was easier to work and often cheaper than natural materials. Cellulose nitrate, the basic constituent of celluloid, was later used as a photographic film base (American invention, 1884), and still later as a fast drying low viscosity lacquer (American invention, 1923). Cellulose nitrate thus served many markets—a typical feature of successful plastics. Galalith, the second plastic, was invented in Germany in 1899. Primarily offered as a cheaper substitute for celluloid, galalith found its greatest application in the button trade. In 1905 Germany introduced cellulose acetate photographic film base, a less flammable substitute for cellulose nitrate film base. Cellulose acetate also served as a lacquer (German invention, 1905) and as a solid plastic (French invention, 1922). In 1909 America introduced the fourth plastic, phenol formaldehyde. Solid phenol formaldehyde enjoyed wide acceptance in the electric appliance industry, because of its resistance to heat and electricity. Resinous phenol formaldehyde served as an adhesive and coating, often superseding animal glues and linseed oil paint.

After World War I new plastics were introduced at a more rapid pace. Cellophane, the famous transparent wrapping, was invented in France during the war, and by 1930 its manufacture had spread to many countries. In 1926 alkyd resins, essential to the rapid finishing of automobiles, were first produced in America. Urea formaldehyde, in many respects a substitute for phenol formaldehyde, was first manufactured by a British firm in 1928; and polyvinyl acetate, an adhesive and emulsion, was jointly introduced in Germany and America the same year. During the early 1930's, Germany invented two of today's largest volume plastics: polystyrene and polyvinyl chloride. Later in the decade, Imperial Chemical Industries (I.C.I.) of Britain invented high pressure polyethylene, another very important plastic.

World War II witnessed the American invention of some speciality plastics: silicone and nylon (1941); polyester (1942); and fluoroethylene (1943). The postwar period has seen the introduction of still more novel plastics: epoxy (Switzerland, 1946); acetal (United States, 1953); linear polyethylene and polypropylene (Italy, 1954 and 1957); and polycarbonate (Germany and America, 1957).

The first synthetic rubber, methyl butadiene, was manufactured by Germany during World War I to counteract the British blockade.[3] Its quality was poor, and production ceased with the end of hostilities. Research was nevertheless carried forward by I.G. Farben, and in 1934 Germany began producing two good synthetic rubbers, styrene and nitrile. A few years earlier Du Pont had introduced neoprene, a special purpose synthetic rubber, in the United States. Shortly after the outbreak of World War II, America and Canada erected vast styrene rubber plants, and these facilities still account for much of the Western World's present synthetic rubber capacity. Following the war, Germany's styrene rubber plants fell into Russian hands. For our purposes, this deprived Germany of her styrene rubber leadership, since our study excludes the Communist World. During the war, however, Germany developed polyurethane rubber (especially suited for foams); the facilities for its manufacture, along with those for nitrile rubber, were fortunately located in the Western zone. In 1944 America introduced silicone rubber, which withstands high temperatures, and in 1951 Du Pont invented hypalon, another speciality rubber. The United States became the first country to manufacture cis-polybutadiene, a rubber chemically identical to natural rubber, in 1958.

Man-made fibre was manufactured as early as 1884 by Count Hilaire de Chardonnet at Besançon, France.[4] Chardonnet's fibre, nitrocellulose rayon, suffered from high flammability, and after a few unfortunate accidents the plant shut down. It was not re-opened until 1891, when a denitration process was discovered to render the fibre less flammable. Vereinigte Glanzstoff Fabriken of Germany introduced cuprammonium rayon, the second man-made fibre, in 1897. In 1900 the Viscose Spinning Syndicate of Britain first produced viscose rayon, soon destined to become the most important man-made fibre. Cellulose acetate fibre was discovered in 1907, but it was not a commercial success until after World War I when British Celanese greatly improved the manufacturing process.

Man-made fibres were initially viewed as "artificial silk" because they were marketed as continuous filaments, very much like natural silk. But the First World War caused a quiet revolution in the industry. Responding to the British blockade Vereinigte Glanzstoff Fabriken sought to manufacture a satisfactory cotton substitute. Cotton, unlike silk, occurs in short lengths called staple. Glanzstoff thus chopped up its continuous rayon filaments to make rayon staple. German textile firms were then able to process this rayon staple with the same methods they had developed for cotton. After the war, man-made fibre producers elsewhere began manufacturing viscose rayon and cellulose acetate staple.

The first new man-made fibre invented after World War I was nylon, introduced in 1938. An American invention, nylon was soon produced by many European countries. During the Second World War, Germany introduced acrylic fibre and Britain invented polyester fibre, both wool substitutes. But polyester fibre was first produced by Du Pont in 1949; a year later I.C.I. commenced manufacture. Polyethylene fibre (Britain, 1951), polypropylene fibre (Italy and America, 1957), and spandex (United States, 1958) are some of the post-war inventions. As indicated by the similarity of nomenclature, the basic chemical materials for many man-made fibres are also used in plastics.

From this condensed survey, one main feature stands out: a very few countries have discovered practically all synthetic materials. America and Germany have dominated the field, followed by Britain, France, and Italy. On an unweighted count, America has 29 innovations to her credit, Germany 22, Britain 4, France 3, and Italy 5. Other countries have 5 in the aggregate.[5] Needless to say, the nations which have contributed most to discovery have also dominated production volume and exports. Table 2–1 documents the commanding position of the leading nations.

The similarity of nomenclature between various plastics, rubbers, and man-made fibres indicates another important feature of the industry: materials with diverse economic uses are sometimes closely related chemically. It is this characteristic which justifies the designation of a synthetic materials "industry". Not only are synthetic materials all produced through chemical processes—vats, tanks, and pipes are typical instruments of production rather than assembly lines or moving machinery—but also nearly all synthetics are high polymer materials. And the investigation of one high polymer often borders very closely on another. W. H. Carother's discovery of nylon (both a plastic and a fibre) laid the groundwork for the discovery of polyester fibre by J. R. Winfield and J. T. Dickson in Britain. Likewise, the I.G. Farben discovery of polystyrene plastic led naturally to the invention of styrene rubber; and I.G. Farben's research on polymethyl methacrylate plastic opened the way to nitrile rubber, which in turn led to acrylic fibre. Indeed, it has now become standard practice for a firm which discovers a new high polymer to investigate its plastic-forming, rubber-forming, and fibre-forming possibilities.

Table 2-1. Production and Exports of Leading Nations as Percent of World Total[a]

	Production				Exports			
	1924	1938	1950	1960	1924	1938	1950	1960
United States	32%	21%	60%	44%	3%	9%	22%	34%
Germany[b]	27%	29%	7%	13%	22%	20%	8%	18%
United Kingdom	13%	7%	9%	9%	19%	8%	17%	12%
France	9%	4%	3%	5%	7%	5%	7%	5%
Italy	9%	11%	3%	5%	21%	32%	10%	9%
Japan	3%	23%	4%	10%	3%	13%	1%	4%
TOTAL	93%	95%	88%	86%	75%	87%	65%	82%

Sources: J. Delorme, *Le Commerce des Matières Plastiques dans le Monde*, 1956; G. S. Whitby, *Synthetic Rubber*, 1954; *Rubber Statistical Bulletin*, *Textile Organon*, OEEC, *Industrial Statistics 1900-1959*, 1950; official production and trade statistics.
   Notes: (*a*) Non-communist world only. Percentages by weight. (*b*) West Germany after 1945.

The technical bonds joining plastics, synthetic rubbers, and man-made fibres are to some extent reflected in the concentration of innovation found among synthetic materials. Due to the chemical similarities of synthetics, one innovation by a given firm almost certainly increases the likelihood of the next. Aside from generating a pertinent body of high polymer research findings, a tradition of innovation attracts the brains and produces the financial success requisite for its own propagation.[6] This is not to say that small firms and inexperienced firms never innovate. Numerous instances may be cited to the contrary.* But the advantage lies with the large and knowledgeable concern. Du Pont, for example, has introduced ten new synthetic materials since 1920. I.G. Farben

* If the small firm combines executive persistence with scientific talent, it may in fact thrive. Starting with a small vat at his New York laboratory, Dr. Leo Baekeland for example built a large industrial empire with subsidiaries in many countries on the basis of his discovery of phenol formaldehyde. Other examples of small innovators are cited in my thesis, *op. cit.*, pp. 61-2. Yet most innovations emanate from the laboratories of established firms. Cf. E. Mansfield, "Size of Firm, Market Structure, and Innovation," *Journal of Political Economy*, December 1963.

was equally fertile during its short life. The huge German combine discovered eleven new synthetics between 1929 and 1943.[7]

Regardless whether the firm is an innovator however, it must normally undertake considerable research before beginning production. Since economies of scale probably characterise research endeavour, this requirement may partially explain the market structures which typify synthetic materials. Oligopoly and monopoly are the rule; competition is the exception. As Table 2–2 suggests, the two leading producers frequently account for as much as half the nation's output.

But market structures are not static. With the dissemination of know-how and the expiration of patents, a market structure typically evolves from monopoly to oligopoly, and perhaps eventually to monopolistic competition. Then, as the product is superseded by newer materials and profits prove less lucrative, the number of firms diminishes. For example, between 1878 and 1896 the Rheinische Gummi- und Zelluloid Fabrik enjoyed a monopoly of the German celluloid industry. In 1901 the industry consisted of five producers, and by 1930 it had expanded to ten or fifteen firms. Competition from newer plastics and economic depression then led to the establishment of a cartel. The British viscose rayon industry furnishes a similar pattern. Courtaulds was the sole producer from 1904 until about 1927. Between 1927 and 1931, eight or ten small firms joined the industry, but most of them subsequently collapsed. Now the British viscose rayon industry consists of only three firms.

Discussions of international commerce often assume perfect competition. From the theoretical viewpoint, however, it is not inappropriate that competition is the exception among synthetic materials. For both the scale economy account and the technological gap account presuppose increasing returns to scale; and competition supplies *prima facie* evidence against scale economies.

Rapid rates of growth have long characterised synthetic materials production. Since 1913, the quantity of world plastics production has regularly increased by 10% to 14% annually. Synthetic rubber production grew explosively during World War II; since 1949 production has advanced about 10% annually. Man-made fibre output was comparatively stagnant before World

Synthetic Materials

Table 2–2. Representative Examples of Market Structure
Capacities in Thousand Metric Tons

1928: Italy, viscose rayon	
Snia Viscosa	10·5
Chatillon	4·8
Snia Varedo	1·8
Enka	0·9
General Viscose	0·3

1933: Japan, viscose rayon	
Teikoku	12·0
Asahi	9·0
Toyo	7·0
Showa	7·2
Kurashiki	5·8
Nippon	4·7
Tokyo	1·8
Japan Woolen	0·6
Mie	0·6

1937: Germany, celluloid	
Rheinische Gummi & Zelluloid	2·4
Deutsche Celluloid	1·9
Celluloidfabrik Speyer	1·6
Kirrmeier & Scherer	0·4
Westfalisch-Anhaltische	0·1

1954: Japan, polyvinyl chloride	
Japanese Geon	7·8
Shin Nippon Chisso Hiryo	4·8
Kanegafuchi	4·8
Monsanto Kasei	4·2
Mitsui	3·6
Sumitomo	3·0
Tekkosha	2·4
Electro-Chemical	2·4
Toa Gosei	0·6
Nippon Carbide	0·6

1958: USA, epoxy	
Shell	16·0
Devoe & Reynolds	4·5
Reichhold	4·5
CIBA	1·8
Union Carbide	1·4
American Marietta	1·1
Dow	0·9

1959: USA, vinyl acetate	
Air Reduction	41·0
Union Carbide: Texas	29·5
New York	13·6
Celanese	22·7
Du Pont	13·6

1958: USA, styrene rubber	
Goodyear Tire	240
Firestone Tire	190
Texas-U.S. Chemical	137
Goodrich-Gulf:	
W. Virginia	122
Texas	95
Shell	110
Phillips	110
American Synthetic Rubber	69
General Tire & Rubber	69
United Carbon	68
U.S. Rubber	30

1960: Brazil, phenol formaldehyde	
Alba	1·3
Plasticos de Brasil	1·0
Resana	0·8
Plastiresana	0·8
Resimbra	0·5
General Electric	0·3
Sacra	0·1

1962: UK, high pressure polyethylene	
I.C.I.	105
Monsanto	30
Union Carbide	24
Petrochemicals (Shell)	15

1962: Germany, linear polyethylene	
Farbwerke Hoechst	34
Rheinische Olefinwerke	12
Chemische Werke Huls	6
Scholvenchemie	6
Ruhrchemie	3

Sources: *Artificial Silk World*, June 28, 1928, and January 1934; R. Rabald, *Die Absatzentwicklung auf dem Deutschen Rohcelluloidmark*, 1951; U.S. Department of Commerce, *World Survey of Plastics*, 1959; W. N. Bowie, *Epoxy Resins*, 1959; *Chemical Engineering*, May 2, 1962; *Chemische Industrie International*, June 1958 and December 1962; private communication from Brazil.

War I. But by 1920 the viscose rayon process had greatly improved, and production increased ten-fold between 1920 and 1930. Since 1930, man-made fibre output has grown about 10% annually.[8]

These growth rates are thrown into perspective by comparison with overall economic growth rates prevailing in North America, Europe, and Japan. Between 1913 and 1960, world synthetic materials production rose from 46,000 metric tons to 10,375,000 metric tons, about 12% a year.[9] By contrast, overall industrial production in the major countries grew little more than 3% annually during this period.[10]

Another way of looking at the synthetic materials boom is through a comparison with competing goods. Aluminium production, at 630,000 metric tons, was twice as large as plastics production in 1939; but at 3,400,000 metric tons, aluminium output was barely 60% of plastics output in 1960. Synthetic rubber was quite unimportant in 1939; at 1,900,000 metric tons in 1960 it had nearly surpassed natural rubber. Man-made fibre output constituted about one-seventh of wool and cotton production before the Second World War, but by 1960 it had doubled this fraction.[11]

High rates of growth in synthetic materials output have been made possible partly by the growth of overall world production, and partly by the ceaseless introduction of new synthetics and constant improvement of older ones. The growth of world production assists the growth of synthetics production simply because each new product has a larger potential market than its predecessor. The increase in number and improvement in quality of synthetic materials extends their effective application range, and thus substantially encourages the industry's expansion.*

The markets for a synthetic material typically develop more rapidly when it is young. For example, from 1913 to 1933, world phenol formaldehyde production increased about 18% annually, while from 1933 to 1953 it increased only 10% annually. From 1940 to 1953, world polyvinyl chloride production grew 25%

---

* Indeed, there is reason to believe that the growth of synthetic materials output has been stimulated much more by these "internal" factors than by the mere growth of demand in other sectors of the economy. On the one hand, there is no evidence that the income elasticity of synthetic materials demand (measured by the cross-section technique) much exceeds unity, while on the other hand, the growth of synthetic materials output has been about four times as great as the growth of world income.

annually, while since 1953 it has advanced about 14% annually. Styrene synthetic rubber production increased (partly under war pressures) 25% annually from 1940 to 1950, and about 10% annually from 1950 to 1960. Likewise, viscose rayon production grew 22% annually from 1920 to 1940, and only 4% annually from 1940 to 1960.

The fact that markets grow most rapidly when a material is young relates to the hypothesis set forth in the technological gap theory regarding static scale economy exploitation. The innovator can confidently erect quite large facilities, knowing that markets will develop to match capacity. Assisted by static scale economies, he can then export to foreign markets. But the imitator, particularly the late imitator, enjoys no such rosy prospect. Markets everywhere are developing more slowly, and the imitator has a difficult task finding the sales outlets to justify a large and economical plant.

Scale Economies. A pioneering article by C. H. Chilton appeared in 1950 on *static* scale economies in capital costs.[12] Chilton assumes that two plants use the same process technology, and that one plant is merely an enlarged version of the other. He then relates plant costs to capacity in an exponential fashion using the general formula:

(1) $\dfrac{K_1}{K_2} = \left[\dfrac{S_1}{S_2}\right]^y$ Where:

K_1, K_2 are capital costs for plants of different size;
S_1, S_2 are capacities of these plants;
y is the plant factor $(0 < y < 1)$.

If different capacities are meaningful alternatives, the "plant factor"[13] for a given process must always fall between zero and unity. A plant factor less than zero would dictate the larger and cheaper plant, even if the additional capacity could not be used; a plant factor greater than unity would dictate parallel small plants rather than a single large plant.

In fact, however, chemical plant factors nearly always lie between one-half and unity. Chilton suggested six-tenths as an approximation in the absence of empirical evidence. According to Chilton's approximation, if a 1,000 metric ton plant costs $3 million, a 5,000 metric ton plant should cost about $8 million.

The existence of exponential scale economies, as opposed to other mathematically feasible types, and the rationale for plant factors lying between one-half and unity both originate in certain fundamental relationships between volume and surface area which apply to chemical plants. Plant capacity is a function of volume, while plant capital cost is a function of surface area. The sphere and the cylinder illustrate these relationships.

As a first approximation, the capital cost of a plant consisting solely of a sphere is the area of sheet steel required to form the sphere, $4\pi r^2$. Its capacity is the volume of the sphere, $(4/3)\pi r^3$. Capital cost and capacity for two plants, one with sphere radius r_1, the other with sphere radius r_2, are therefore:

$$(2) \quad \frac{4\pi r_1^2}{4\pi r_2^2} = \left[\frac{(4/3)\pi r_1^3}{(4/3)\pi r_2^3}\right]^y$$

The plant factor required to establish equality, after the manner of equation (1), is denoted y. If equation (2) is reduced by cancellation, it becomes apparent that y must be two-thirds. A plant factor of two-thirds also applies to the cube.

Now consider a plant consisting solely of a cylinder. If plant capacity is expanded only by enlarging the radius of the cylinder while leaving its height intact, and if end surfaces are unimportant, the plant factor is one-half. This can be seen by comparing the formula for cylinder surface area (excluding end surfaces), $2\pi rh$, with the formula for cylinder volume, $\pi r^2 h$. The cylinder is perhaps the most commonly found chemical processing equipment shape (pipes, vats, columns, tanks), which explains why plant factors are sometimes as low as one-half. Indeed, one-half is the lowest possible plant factor arising from volume : surface relationships, provided that equipment is expanded without being altered in shape.

The analogy of spheres and cylinders applies fairly well to plastic and synthetic rubber plants, and to the facilities for making intermediate chemicals which are used in manufacturing most synthetic materials. But the analogy breaks down when it comes to man-made fibre spinning plants. A spinning plant is typically expanded via repetition; more spinnerets and winding spools are installed rather than enlarging each spool or piercing additional holes in each spinneret. As a result, plant factors are close to unity, and there are few capital scale economies. However, the extensive chemical processes which precede the actual spinning of filaments do exhibit the usual capital scale economies.

Table 2–3 presents some plant factors drawn from American experience. The data largely applies to intermediate chemicals

Table 2–3.   Plant Factors drawn from American Experience

Product (ancillary material or process)	Plant Factor	Labour Factor
INTERMEDIATE CHEMICALS		
Ethylene (ex ethane or propane)	.67	.20
Chlorine (ex salt; diaphragm process)	.75	.22
Hydrochloric Acid (ex chlorine)	.70	.22
Hydrated Lime (ex limestone)	.70	.22
Ethylene Glycol (chlorohydrin or oxidation process)	.63	.22
Ethylene Oxide (chlorohydrin or oxidation process)	.63	.22
Acetylene (ex ethane; Wulff process)	.60	.15
Ammonia (ex fuel oil)	.80	.40
Hydrocyanic Acid (ex methane and ammonia)	.70	.20
Sulfuric Acid (ex sulfur)	.85	.22
Nitric Acid (ex ammonia)	.63	.20
Urea (ex ammonia)	.67	.20
Benzene (ex refinery hydrocarbons)	na	.20
Sodium Cyanide (ex hydrocyanic acid and caustic soda)	.65	.22
Butadiene (ex butane)	.65	.22
Tetrahydrofuran (ex furfural)	na	.22
Adipic Acid (ex cyclohexane; air or nitric acid oxidation process)	na	.22
Adiponitrile (ex tetrahydrofuran or butadiene or adipic acid)	na	.22
PLASTIC		
Vinyl Chloride Monomer (ex ethylene or acetylene)	.72	.20
Polyvinyl Chloride (ex vinyl chloride monomer)	.70	na
Styrene (ex ethylene and benzene)	.50	na
High Pressure or Linear Polyethylene (ex ethylene)	.65	na
Polypropylene (ex propylene)	.65	na
SYNTHETIC RUBBERS		
Styrene Rubber (ex styrene, butadiene)	.65	.20
MAN-MADE FIBRES		
All Fibre Spinning (ex chemical solutions)	1.0	1.0

Sources: W. Isard, *et al.*, *Industrial Complex Analysis*, 1959; *European Chemical News*, March 2, March 9, 1962; *Chemical Engineering*, October, 1955; private sources. (na) not available.

used in the production of synthetic materials.* Normally the firm would manufacture these intermediate chemicals as well as combining them to produce the synthetic material itself. But capital scale economies are not peculiar to the materials itemised in Table 2–3. They are rooted in fundamental relation-

---

* Unfortunately the youthful character of many synthetic materials militates against publication of similar economic data regarding their plant factors.

ships just as applicable to the infant celluloid industry of 1870 as to the developed industries of today. In this connection, it is interesting to observe that the relationship between aggregate invested capital and total output in the American, Japanese, and Canadian plastics industries corroborates Chilton's approximation of a six-tenths plant factor.[14]

Largely for the sake of symmetry, it has been suggested that static labour scale economies, like capital scale economies, should be cast in an exponential form:[15]

$$(3) \quad \frac{L_1}{L_2} = \left[\frac{S_1}{S_2}\right]^z$$

Where: L_1, L_2 are man-years required to run different sized plant; S_1, S_2 are capacities of these plants; z is the labour factor ($0 < z < 1$).

It has also been suggested that labour scale economies ordinarily exceed capital scale economies by a substantial margin.[16] A typical chemical plant has a fixed number of "joints", and it is argued that each joint requires the attention of a single labourer, pretty much regardless of its size. Some labour activities, such as warehousing, may increase directly with capacity, but they are in the minority. Hence "labour factors" may be as low as three-tenths, which is very low indeed: if a 1,000-ton plant required 100 production workers, a 5,000-ton plant would require only 160 workers. Although such extensive labour scale economies have been suggested by persuasive authority, they are not supported by international labour comparisons. Diagrams 2–1 and 2–2 chart plastics and man-made fibre output against total labour force in a variety of countries for 1960 (except where otherwise noted). The diagrams indicate a six-tenths or seven-tenths labour factor.* That is to say, they seem to show that labour scale economies are approximately the same magnitude as capital scale economies.

Perhaps in small countries plants are bigger, relative to total output, than in large countries, and as a result the labour factors derived from Diagrams 2–1 and 2–2 do not fully reflect actual

---

* In Diagram 2–2, Austria and Sweden are separated from the other countries because these two nations concentrate very heavily on staple fibre as opposed to continuous filament; and staple fibre requires less labour per ton of output than continuous filament.

scale economies.* But whether or not labour scale economies are greater than these diagrams would indicate, capital and labour scale economies taken together are certainly large enough to substantially affect the course of trade.

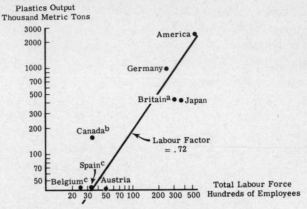

Diagram 2–1. Employment in Plastics Production

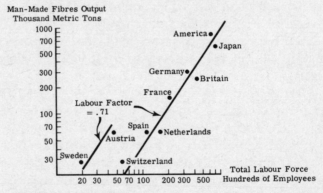

Diagram 2–2. Employment in Man-Made Fibres Production

Sources: OEEC, *The Chemical Industry in Europe;* official censuses of production; private communications from OEEC.

Notes: (a) 1958. (b) 1959. (c) 1961. Unless otherwise noted, the data pertains to 1960. Labour factors estimated by least squares.

It should be emphasised that the static scale economies just discussed are only harvested when a larger version of a particular

* Dow-Unquinesa, for example, supplies a larger share of the Spanish plastics market than its parent firm, Dow Chemical, claims of the United States plastics market. On the other hand, countries with greater total output might require less labour to run a given sized plant, due to dynamic scale economies. Thus it could be argued that the labour factors estimated from Diagrams 2–1 and 2–2 tend to exaggerate actual static labour scale economies.

systems achieve a high degree of perfection, and major economies are realised in the use of raw materials.

British Xylonite's experience with polystyrene illustrates the second type of progress, higher process speeds. When British Xylonite installed its polymerisation plant in 1952, the plant had a rated capacity of 2,000 metric tons per year. Ten years later, with minor physical modifications and excellent engineering improvements, the plant's capacity had been boosted to 16,000 metric tons per year.[23] If we visualise a typical chemical plant as a cylinder, then the plant's capacity depends both upon the dimensions of the cylinder and the speed with which the cylinder processes raw materials into finished product. If the cylinder's dimensions are enlarged, static scale economies are harvested. But if higher process speeds result from greater familiarity with the cylinder's behaviour, then dynamic scale economies are reaped. As British Xylonite's experience shows, the economies in capital and labour usage achieved through higher process speeds may far exceed the static scale economies which might be obtained through erecting a larger plant.

We may profitably mention a few other examples of improved process speeds. The styrene monomer plants constructed for the American styrene rubber programme during World War II initially operated on a batch basis. Later continuous processing became possible. As a result, capacities were significantly expanded without additional capital outlays. Thus, when the Texas City styrene monomer plant was built in 1946, it had a rated capacity of 45,000 metric tons. At the time of a disastrous fire in 1947, it was said to have a capacity of 90,000 metric tons.[24]

In the viscose rayon industry, higher process speeces have been achieved through a variety of mechanical and chemical improvements. Prominent among these are faster revolution of the spinning pot which winds viscose rayon, and reduced time for ripening the viscose solution before spinning it into fibre. By such improvements, United States viscose rayon output per manhour was substantially increased in the decade from 1923 to 1933. Output in 1923 was 0·41 kg. per man-hour; in 1925, 0·44 kg.; in 1927, 0·49 kg.; in 1929, 0·53 kg.; in 1931, 0·80 kg.; and in 1933, 1·06 kg.[25, 26]

It was mentioned earlier that intertemporal and international comparisons furnish tentative support for Kaldor's version of the dynamic scale economy hypothesis. When a plant is freshly commissioned, estimates often appear in the trade press of its capital cost and capacity. These estimates not only reflect the size of the plant, but also the process speeds attained. The influence of static scale economies (plant size) may be eliminated by applying a six-tenths "plant factor" to find the equivalent cost of a plant of some standard size, say 10,000 metric tons.[27] The remaining differences in costs per ton of capacity—that is, differences in process speeds—should be correlated with the length of time the country has been manufacturing the product. Specifically, the capital cost should decline as the length of experience increases.*

Diagrams 2–3, 2–4, 2–5 and 2–6 confirm this prediction. These diagrams are based on statistics presented in Appendix Tables C–20 through C–23. Plant costs per metric ton of output—adjusted for static scale economies—are graphed against the number of years the country had been in production as of 1962. 1962 was chosen as the cut-off date, since most plants under consideration were put on stream during the period 1960–64. When more than one plant (for which data was available) had been commissioned in a given country during the 1960–64 period, the capital requirements of the various plants were averaged to obtain a single figure for the nation.

Clearly, capital costs for high pressure polyethylene, polypropylene, polyvinyl chloride, and styrene monomer (used in styrene rubber and polystyrene) declined, as predicted, with production experience. These are the only four synthetics on which adequate comparative data could be found; but that data presents a reasonably convincing picture.

To be sure, the correlations are not perfect. Considering their production experience, as measured by the length of time in production, Sweden, Denmark, and South Africa show unusually low capital costs in polyethylene production. Two extraneous

---

* This formulation does not allow for the fact that a country with 5 years of prior experience which begins production in 1965 will almost certainly achieve higher process speeds than a country with 5 years of prior experience which began production in 1940. But such allowance is unnecessary when all the plants under consideration were erected at about the same time, as is true of our sample groups.

explanations might be offered for these observations. First, native engineering sophistication (particularly in Sweden) may partly compensate for a lack of actual production experience. Second, the plants in these three countries were built by subsidiaries of I.C.I. and Union Carbide, two of the oldest and best established firms in the polyethylene business. Similarly, Japanese costs of erecting a styrene monomer plant seem rather low in view of

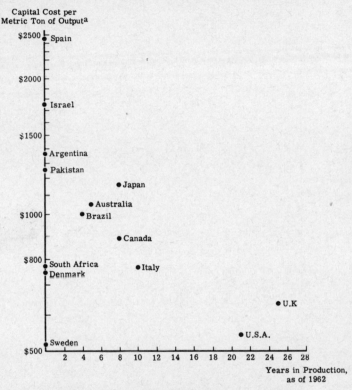

Diagram 2-3. High Pressure Polyethylene Plant Costs
Note: (a) Adjusted for static scale economies.
Source: Appendix Table C-20.

Japanese production experience. Again, two special considerations should be mentioned. First, Japan worked with synthetic rubbers during World War II, but since production ceased with the end of hostilities, 1960 is cited as the beginning date of Japanese styrene monomer production. This procedure may understate Japan's actual experience.[28] Second, Japanese construction costs are very low, quite apart from any superiority in building styrene monomer plants. One source suggests that Japan can build an entirely equivalent plant for 65% of United States construction costs.[29]

But it deserves emphasis that even without these *ad hoc* explanations—which in the main merely assert that length of time in pro-

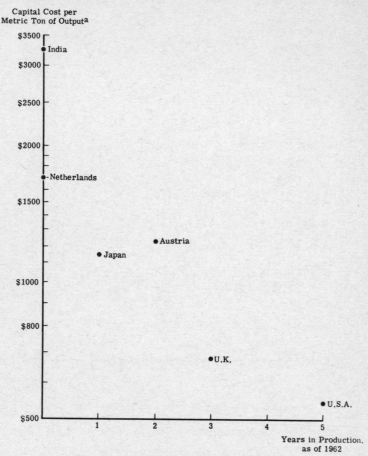

Diagram 2–4.   Polypropylene Plant Costs
Note: (*a*) Adjusted for static scale economies.
Source: Appendix Table C–21.

duction is not a comprehensive measure of production experience —the diagrams offer support for Kaldor's version of the dynamic scale economy hypothesis. Moreover, if we assume that home market size is a reasonable proxy for accumulated volume of past production, then the correlation between capital costs and time in production works out rather better than the correlation between capital costs and production volume. The interested reader can demonstrate this for himself by contrasting the data in these diagrams with the data in Appendix Table C–7.

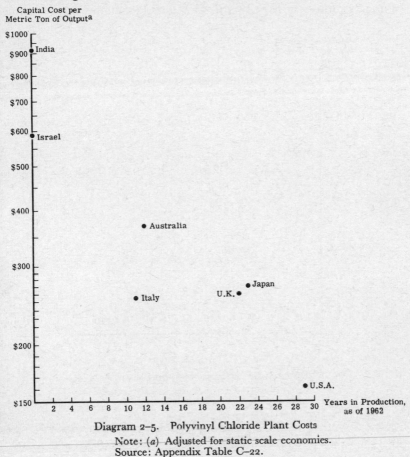

Diagram 2–5. Polyvinyl Chloride Plant Costs

Note: (a) Adjusted for static scale economies.
Source: Appendix Table C–22.

Pricing Behaviour. Innovating firms are not normally content to earn average profits on their new synthetic materials. New products are instead priced, whenever possible, to earn generous rewards in their first years. Of necessity, smaller returns are yielded as the product grows older. Diagram 2–7 illustrates the idealized price behaviour and the associated profit pattern.[30] This diagram presupposes that differences between new synthetics and existing materials allow innovating producers some freedom in establishing prices. With the exception of styrene synthetic rubber, this presupposition has normally been true.

Some examples of the high profits reaped by the early producers of new synthetics may be useful. For the first seven years of United

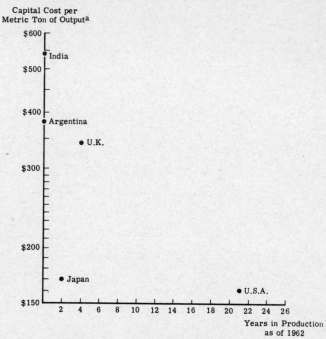

Diagram 2–6.   Styrene Monomer Plant Costs
Note: (*a*) Adjusted for static scale economies.
Source: Appendix Table C–23.

States polyethylene manufacture, prices remained above $1·00 per kilogram, and profit margins probably yielded a 50% return on fixed capital after taxes.[31] Similarly, profits in the American viscose rayon industry yielded at least 30% annually on invested capital prior to 1925;[32] by all accounts, profits were equally generous in other countries.[33] Likewise, profits on cellophane manufacture in the United States probably exceeded 40% on fixed capital until 1932.[34] And the substantial internal growth of

pioneering firms such as I.C.I., Bayer, Montacatini, Rhone-
Poulenc, Du Pont, and Toyo Rayon during the past forty years
bears ample testimony to the rewards conferred upon early
producers.

Prices on international markets should be expected to fall,
with the passage of time, simply because low-wage producers are
continually entering, and disturbing, the market. According to the
technological gap account, high-wage countries introduce most

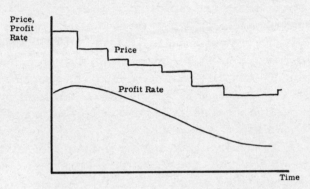

Diagram 2–7. Idealised Price and Profit Behaviour

new commodities. Thus, successive producing countries are almost
bound to have lower labour costs, which will eventually be translated into overall lower production costs. But why should prices
and profits fall in a domestic market which is more or less insulated from international trade?

One reason is that established producers do not ordinarily set
prices with a view to excluding new entrants. Instead they
apparently prefer to rely upon legal protection and secrecy to
serve that purpose. Competition is thus invited, and prices and
profits fall in consequence. For example, in 1952 the American
courts compelled I.C.I. to license its polyethylene technology to
other firms besides Union Carbide and Du Pont. Six new producers entered the market within three years, and another three
by 1961.[35] Clearly the pricing policies of the duopolists prior to
1952 did not deter new entrants. However, under the weight of
fresh competition prices fell from $1·00 per kilogram in 1952 to

about $0·60 per kilogram in 1960. Likewise, when the Bakelite Company's key patents on phenol formaldehyde expired in 1926, the American industry was rapidly transformed from a monopoly to monopolistic competition: by 1937, 36 firms were offering phenol formaldehyde in one form or another.[36] Moreover, prices fell from approximately $1·10 per kilogram to $0·45 per kilogram during this period.[37]

It may seem peculiar that initial producers do not lower prices to a level which would preclude new competition. For if they choose to use their static and dynamic scale economies as blunt instruments for excluding other firms, market structures might never leave the monopoly stage. But judging from the examples cited above and in Table 2–1, large established producers rarely do use pricing policy for restricting entry. The question is why they do not. This is a challenging question, but since our study does not focus on the complexities of oligopoly pricing behaviour, we shall not attempt to answer it.

A second reason why prices fall in an insulated domestic market is that established producers may wish to expand total profits at the expense of profit margins. When a synthetic material is first introduced, it frequently competes with only one or two existing goods, because its price is high. As prices are reduced, new markets become feasible, and sales mount. Profit rates fall, but total profits may increase. The American cellophane industry offers an excellent example of this behaviour. In the United States, cellophane has always been produced by a very small number of firms. From 1924 until 1929, Du Pont enjoyed a monopoly; in 1929 Sylvania Industrial Corp. began production; and not until 1951 did a third producer, Olin Mathieson, enter the market. This high degree of concentration resulted from patent protection and technological secrecy. Yet between 1924 and 1946, prices were reduced substantially. An American trial court found that prices were not lowered with the aim of precluding new competition. Rather:[38]

> each price reduction was intended to open up new uses for cellophane, and to attract new customers who had not used cellophane because of its price.

There is a third reason why prices are progressively lowered, wholly apart from any reduction of profit margins. The presence of scale economies means that production costs can be substantially reduced over time. Higher process speeds, raw materials savings, and larger plants may all contribute to lower costs. And if these economies are passed on, prices can be cut without reducing profit margins.

Aside from events within the particular industry, prices and profits may be forced down by external events. More specifically, the appearance of new and superior products will at some stage affect the trade. By 1930 phenol formaldehyde, for example, was exerting considerable pressure upon celluloid prices; nylon had the same effect upon viscose rayon after World War II; and cis-polybutadiene rubber will eventually curb the profits on styrene rubber.

From the viewpoint of the technological gap nature-of-trade theory, initial high profits are the most important feature of pricing behaviour. Without these profits, foreign firms might have little incentive to undertake the manufacture of new synthetic materials. For even though synthetic rubbers and man-made fibres compete directly with natural commodities, the producers of such commodities have not often responded to the obvious threat by undertaking synthetics production at home. The usual reaction has rather been to proclaim the virtues of nature's commodities. Brazil in 1960 became the first rubber producer to manufacture styrene synthetic rubber (nineteen years after America), and even then the initiative was taken by chemical concerns rather than plantation owners. Similarly, firms engaged in producing natural fibres have seldom introduced man-made fibres production (the Japanese silk industry is a notable exception). And since the typical plastic competes with many commodities, it is unlikely that any particular firm will even view the imports of new plastics as a major threat. These observations suggest that high profits, rather than threatened markets, largely motivate the spread of synthetic materials manufacture from one nation to another.*

* Perhaps this generalisation requires modification once a synthetic materials industry has become established. For example, the threat which nylon poses to viscose rayon may, by itself, stimulate viscose rayon firms to undertake nylon production.

It may be useful to conclude by reviewing the experience of nitrocellulose rayon, the pioneer man-made fibre. Nitrocellulose rayon was first produced by Count Chardonnet at Besançon in 1884.[39] The initial product easily caught fire, and manufacture was temporarily discontinued. But the factory was reopened in 1891, and "by 1895 was earning huge profits".[40] In 1898 the Chardonnet firm paid its maiden dividend of $6\frac{1}{2}\%$. By 1904 the dividend had increased to 150%, marking the peak of prosperity. In 1905 the dividend was reduced to 60%, and in 1906 and 1907 only 30% was paid. In 1908 no dividend was declared.[41] From this point, nitrocellulose rayon began to slip from pre-eminence. As one writer commented:[42]

> This state of affairs was due, in the first instance, to the appearance of cuprammonium silk, which was cheaper to produce, and soon after that to the appearance of the still cheaper viscose silk. . . . The procedure of the large cellulose nitrate silk works is now so technically perfect that their yarns can be sold at the same price, or at only slightly higher prices, than viscose silk. . . . Nevertheless, this does not alter the fact that the cellulose nitrate process for the manufacture of artificial silk is doomed to become extinct eventually.

These words were written about 1927 when viscose rayon was still selling for $2·00 per kilogram in Europe. Viscose rayon prices soon fell to about $1·30 per kilogram, which doomed nitrocellulose rayon. However, a few European factories marketed small quantities until World War II, and a plant continued to operate in Brazil until 1948.

In their prime, nitrocellulose profits were sufficiently generous to encourage manufacture wherever the know-how was available. For this reason, Count Chardonnet's advice was very much sought after by potential foreign producers. With Chardonnet's assistance, plants were opened in Germany, Belgium and Switzerland.[43] Later Italy and Japan acquired the necessary technology. By 1930 competition from these two low-wage producers, plus the impact of newer fibres, reduced rewards on nitrocellulose manufacture to unprofitable levels in most countries.

REFERENCES

1. Appendix Table C–3 lists the products and their principal sub-forms.

2. C. A. Redfarn, *A Guide to Plastics*, 1958, is useful on the development of the industry but the information presented here comes from a number of sources. See Appendix A of my thesis, *Synthetic Materials: A Study in International Trade*, 1963 (Cambridge University Library).

3. D. W. Huke, *Introduction to Natural and Synthetic Rubbers*, 1961, and G. S. Whitby, editor, *Synthetic Rubber*, 1954, are both good from the historical viewpoint. Also see Appendix A of my thesis, *op. cit.*

4. D. C. Hague, *Economics of Man-Made Fibres*, 1957, and H. R. Mauersberger, editor, *Matthew's Textile Fibres*, 1954, furnish a good background on the man-made fibres industry. Also see Appendix A of my thesis, *op. cit.*

5. By this count, the total number of innovations exceeds the number of materials listed in Appendix Table C–3. When two countries both began producing in the same year, each is counted as an innovator.

6. M. V. Posner, "International Trade and Technical Change", *Oxford Economic Papers*, October 1961, might describe these self-perpetuating mechanisms as dynamic scale economies to the firm.

7. See my thesis, *op. cit.*, p. 60.

8. See Appendix Table C–19, and the sources cited there.

9. *Ibid.*

10. *National Institute Economic Review*, July 1961.

11. Appendix Table C 19; O.E.E.C., *Industrial Statistics 1900–1959*, 1960; *Rubber Statistical Bulletin*, August 1963; U.N., *Statistical Yearbook*, 1961.

12. C. H. Chilton, "Six-tenths Factor Applies to Complete Plant Costs", *Chemical Engineering*, April 1950. Also see W. Isard, *et al.*, *Industrial Complex Analysis and Regional Development*, 1959, pp. 52–56; and F. T. Moore, "Economies of Scale: Some Statistical Evidence", *Quarterly Journal of Economics*, May 1959.

13. The use of the word "factor" in this context should be distinguished from its use when designating capital or labour *per se*.

14. See Table 5–2, p. 156, Diagram 5–1, p. 158, and the accompanying discussion in my thesis, *op. cit.*

15. W. Isard, *et al.*, *op. cit.*, pp. 54–58.

16. *Ibid.*

17. The firm may still harvest static scale economies in the use of overhead labour; cf. W. Isard, *et al.*, *op. cit.*, pp. 58–61.

18. M. V. Posner, *op. cit.*; K. J. Arrow, "The Economic Implications of Learning by Doing", *Review of Economic Studies*, July 1962; N. Kaldor, "Comment", *Review of Economic Studies*, July 1962.

19. See pp. 27–28.

20. A. N. Shimmin, "The Economic Problems of the Rayon Industry", *Artificial Silk World*, June 28, 1929.

21. Masselon, Roberts, and Cillard, *Celluloid; Its Manufacture, Applications and Substitutes*, 1912, pp. 10–20.

22. United States vs. Du Pont, *118 Federal Supplement 41*, 1954.

23. Private communication.

24. *Modern Plastics*, May 1947.

25. J. Markham, *Competition in the Rayon Industry*, 1952, p. 175.

26. J. L. Enos' study of the petroleum industry, "Invention and Innovation in the Petroleum Refining Industry", in Universities-National Bureau Committee for Economic Research, *The Rate and Direction of Inventive Activity*, 1962, offers much further evidence as to the importance of process improvements. Enos divides industrial discovery into an alpha phase, representing inventive activity preceding introduction of a new product, and a beta phase, representing subsequent process (and product) improvements. In the petroleum industry economic cost-cutting during the beta phase was fully as great as cost-cutting during the alpha phase.

27. See above, pp. 46–48.

28. Chapter 5 sets forth the rationale for this procedure.

29. See Table 3–2.

30. In addition to the points mentioned in the text, Diagram 2–7 suggests two features which sometimes characterise price–profit patterns. First, profits may rise during the initial years as major difficulties in plant operation are overcome. Second, when the product is very old, technological progress may not keep pace with wage increases, and prices may rise.

31. Estimated from data supplied by H. Saechtling, and cost information in *European Chemical News*, March 9, 1962.

32. J. Markham, *Competition in the Rayon Industry*, 1952, Chart 16.

33. For example, see D. C. Hague, *The Economics of Man-Made Fibres*, 1957, on the experience of Courtaulds in Britain.

34. Estimated from A. D. H. Kaplan, *et al.*, *Pricing in Big Business*, 1958; and United States vs. Du Pont, *118 Federal Supplement 41*, 1954.

35. T. O. J. Kresser, *Polyethylene*, 1957; *Chemische Industrie International*, December 1962.

36. U.S. Tariff Commission, *Synthetic Resins and their Raw Materials*, 1938, p. 11.

37. *Op. cit.*, p. 131.

38. Quoted in A. D. H. Kaplan, *et al.*, *Pricing in Big Business*, 1958, p. 100.

39. At about the same time, Chardonnet also helped establish a nitrocellulose rayon factory in Germany. A. H. Hard, *The Rayon Year Book*, 1948.

40. *Op. cit.*, p. 139.

41. F. Reinthaler, *Artificial Silk*, 1928, p. 242.

42. *Ibid.*

43. A. H. Hard, *op. cit.*

Chapter 3

THE FACTOR PROPORTIONS ACCOUNT

THE factor proportions theory asserts that international wage: profit ratio differences decide comparative advantage, and hence the direction in which trade flows. Wage : profit ratio differences can only determine trading patterns, however, if there are no returns to scale and if all countries enjoy approximately the same technology. Among synthetic materials, neither of these assumptions bears up under examination. We have already seen that substantial static and dynamic scale economies characterise the industry. Were it not for these economies, low-wage countries would enjoy a comparative advantage in production. That is to say, if the assumptions of the factor proportions account were approximately fulfilled, low-wage countries would supply most synthetic materials exports. The factor proportions theory thus predicts a trade pattern diametrically opposed to the experience of the twentieth century. Let us see how this result comes about.

Wage Rates, Profit Rates, and Capital Intensities. Appendix Table C–6 presents approximate chemical wage costs (production workers only)[1] in a number of countries for selected years since 1938. Wage costs are expressed in United States dollars per man-year at current exchange rates.

Profit rates are much more difficult to ascertain than wage rates. Since the Second World War, American profit rates on fixed investment in the chemical industry have averaged between 20% and 30% before taxes, after making allowance for depreciation and obsolescence.[2] An authoritative source suggests that medium-risk chemicals should earn at least 25% return on capital investment before taxes.[3] We shall therefore assume that the American synthetic materials industry is not satisfied unless it receives 25%.

Unfortunately little useful statistical data can be found on profit rates outside the United States. A recent theoretical article reported that in 1954 the rate of return on capital in the basic chemical industry was 21% in the United States, 21% in Canada, 24% in Japan, and 22% in India.[4] These figures certainly give no evidence of the major differences in profit rates between countries which the equal technology assumption of the factor proportions theory would require.*

Nevertheless, for the sake of analysis, let us assume that in a country paying a 1960 wage of about $1,000 per man-year (such as Japan or Mexico) the minimum satisfactory before-tax profit rate on synthetic materials production is 40% on fixed capital. Let us moreover assume that every $1,000 increase in the 1962 annual wage brings a 4% decline in the profit rate. Thus, at the 1962 American wage level ($4,900 per man-year), the minimum satisfactory profit is about 25%, as already stipulated. This inverse schedule of wage and profit rates no doubt exaggerates the differences found in the real world. It thereby agrees quite generously with the suppositions of the factor proportions account.

Table 3-1. Approximate Capital Employed per Man

U.S. Industry in 1960

Plastics	$22,000
Synthetic Rubbers	$34,000
Man-Made Fibres	$15,000

Sources: W. W. Leontief, "Factor Proportions and the Structure of American Trade", *Review of Economics and Statistics*, November 1956; U.S. Department of Commerce, *Census of Manufactures*, 1958, and *1960 Annual Survey of Manufactures*, 1962.

Table 3-1 gives rough capital per man estimates for the United States synthetic materials industries in 1960.[5] (We assume that these figures also apply to 1962.) The estimates were derived by adding net capital expenditures between 1947 and 1960 to the 1947 capital per man estimates published by Leontief.[6] Gross capital expenditures were taken from census data; a deduction then had to be made for obsolescence.[7] The resulting figures were further adjusted for inflation between 1947 and 1960,[8] before arriving at the final estimates.

* The incidence of taxation adds a further reason for not anticipating major before-tax profit rate differences between nations. For it is usually true that the poorer the country, the smaller the reliance placed on profits taxes; hence, the same before-tax profit typically yields a higher after-tax return in the less well-to-do nation.

If low-wage countries could extensively substitute labour for capital in producing synthetic materials, we should have to adjust the American capital per man figures to correspond to different wage rates before comparing production costs between nations. However, the high engineering costs of designing a chemical plant strongly militate against redesigning it to employ more labour and less capital. Although some factor substitution may exist, we shall assume that factor substitution is not terribly important in manufacturing synthetic materials.*

Nonetheless, owing to different construction costs, the *same* plant may be cheaper to erect in low-wage countries. Table 3–2,

Table 3–2. Approximate Indices of Chemical Plant Costs

	United States = 100
United States	100
Germany	90- 94
United Kingdom	90- 94
France	95-101
Italy	83- 87
Japan	65- 85
Netherlands	88- 92
Australia	95-105
India	75- 95

Source: Private communication, Dow Chemical Co.

furnished by a leading chemical company, suggests that 1960 plant costs at prevailing exchange rates were lower in Europe than in the United States, and lower in the Far East than in Europe. Indeed, the equal technology assumption of the factor proportions account requires some decrease in plant costs as wage rates decline. For if the highly labour-intensive construction industry is equally efficient in all countries, then plant costs are bound to be

---

* To be sure, capital : labour ratios are doubtless much lower outside the United States. But this has little to do with true factor substitution. Capital : labour ratios primarily vary on account of static scale economies (see footnote 10, Chapter 1), and technological differences. Japanese producers would gladly employ nearly the same capital per man as American producers, if only they enjoyed access to the same markets and methods.

smaller where wage rates are lower. As a crude approximation to the relationship between wage rates and plant costs, let us assume that at the 1962 $1,000 wage level, plant costs were 80% of American plant costs, and that plant costs rose 5% with every $1,000 increase in wage rates.

The Theory Evaluated. The factor proportions theory can now be assessed as an explanation of 1962 synthetic materials trade. This theory, like any other nature-of-trade theory, implies that comparative advantages are transformed into absolute money advantages at equilibrium exchange rates.* Hence if factor prices are expressed in a common currency, and allowance is made for international plant cost differences, it should be possible to predict trade patterns from the absolute money advantages which emerge. The stage has been set for this exercise by: (1) expressing 1962 wage costs in American dollars at current exchange rates (Appendix Table C–6); (2) stipulating an inverse schedule of profit and wage rates—a schedule which seems quite generous to the factor proportions theory; (3) estimating United States capital intensities (Table 3–1); (4) stipulating a direct relationship between wage rates and plant costs (based on Table 3–2).

Diagram 3–1 now charts the annual sum of 1962 wage costs and profit charges per man (i.e., value added per man) against the inverse schedule of wages and profit rates. The lines indicating value added per man-year in Diagram 3–1 differ from price lines for synthetic materials output per man-year only by a constant. That constant is the cost of raw materials, depreciation, and obsolescence.[9] For the factor proportions theory assumes equal technology and no scale economies; consequently, output per man-year will be the same everywhere except for minor differences arising from true factor substitution.

Under the assumptions of the factor proportions account, Diagram 3–1 thus reflects the minimum prices at which synthetic materials can be offered by various countries. Australian chemical

---

* If exchange rates were initially set so that one country could produce all goods more cheaply than other countries—that is, if one country enjoyed an absolute money advantage in the production of all goods—then that country would experience a balance of payments surplus. Exchange rates would have to be readjusted until each country's comparative advantage emerged as an absolute money advantage. Otherwise balance of payments disequilibria would persist.

firms, for example, must pay an annual wage of $2,000. At this wage it is assumed that the minimum satisfactory profit rate is 36%. American plastics factories employ, on the average, $22,000 capital per man. Owing to lower construction labour costs, however, Australian factories employ only $18,700 capital per man (85% of $22,000). Therefore the minimum satisfactory value added in Australian plastics production is $8,700 per man-year. Of this sum, $2,000 must be paid in wages, while the remaining $6,700 is allotted for profits. Australian manufacturers can consequently offer a man-year of plastics output for $8,700 plus the cost of raw materials, depreciation, and obsolescence.

The remarkable feature about Diagram 3–1 is that low-wage countries appear to enjoy an advantage over high-wage countries in the production of all synthetic materials.[10] This feature is

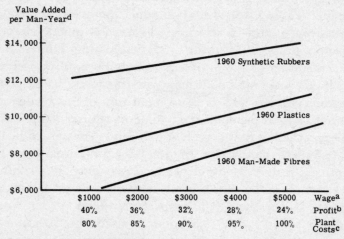

Diagram 3–1.   Value Added per Man Year vs. Wage and Other Costs
(*a*) In United States dollars at current exchange rates.
(*b*) As annual return on fixed investment, before taxes but after obsolescence and depreciation.
(*c*) As percentage of United States plant costs.
(*d*) Sum of profit and wage costs per man-year in United States dollars.

shown by the upward slope, from left to right, in the value added lines, and hence the increase in national offering prices of synthetic materials as wage levels rise. Presumably, then, low-wage countries should supply the larger part of synthetic materials exports. Yet we know from Chapter 2 that the converse is true: high-wage countries provide most synthetic materials exports. Indeed, the truly low-wage countries of Africa, Asia, and Latin America rely almost entirely upon imports for their consumption of synthetic materials.

Diagram 3–1 strongly suggests that the factor proportions theory is not relevant to synthetic materials trade. For if the theory were correct, this diagram would portray high-wage countries as having a substantial money advantage—particularly since synthetic materials are highly capital-intensive goods. The unfavourable implications of Diagram 3–1 are not confined to present-day experience. The same anomalous results emerge when similar calculations are applied to 1938, 1950, and, in all likelihood, other years.[11]

The trouble originates, of course, with the dual assumptions—equal technology and constant returns to scale—underlying the factor proportions theory. The simple truth is that high-wage countries more than compensate for higher wage rates with physical economies in capital and labour usage. If Diagram 3–1 took these economies into consideration, high-wage countries would be credited with the proper advantage in synthetic materials production. Clearly our remaining chapters must attempt to incorporate these crucial economies into a coherent explanation of trade.

REFERENCES

1. Data on salaried employees are not generally available. The data which can be found, however, suggest that if salaried employees were included in Appendix Table C–6 the wage spread between rich and poor countries would be widened.

2. U.S. Federal Trade Commission, *Rates of Return for Identical Companies in Selected Manufacturing Industries, 1940, 1947–60*, 1962. Corporate taxation reduces the range of profit rates by about a fourth.

3. R. S. Aries, R. D. Newton, *Chemical Engineering Cost Estimation*, 1950, p. 93.

4. K. J. Arrow, *et al.*, "Capital-Labor Substitution and Economic Efficiency", *Review of Economics and Statistics*, August 1961.

5. These estimates refer to all employees, not just production workers. As a result, they are on a slightly different footing than the wage figures in Appendix Table C–6.

6. W. W. Leontief, "Factor Proportions and the Structure of American Trade", *Review of Economics and Statistics*, November 1956.

7. A 10% annual obsolescence allowance was applied to the plastics and man-made fibres industries, but only 5% was allowed for synthetic rubber. The difference arises because styrene synthetic rubber has maintained its commanding position since World War II, whereas the plastics and man-made fibres industries have witnessed a more rapid turnover of products.

8. The U.S. Department of Labour's price index for all machinery and motive products was employed. This index is published in U.S. Department of Commerce, *Business Statistics*, 1961.

9. Relying on the discussion of transport charges in Chapter 1 and Appendix A, we assume that raw material costs are the same in all countries. Moreover, there is no reason for expecting depreciation or obsolescence costs to vary radically between nations.

10. The apparent advantage of low-wage countries would, of course, be enhanced if we allowed for factor substitution.

11. See pp. 131–2 of my thesis, *Synthetic Materials: A Study in International Trade*, 1963 (Cambridge University Library).

Chapter 4

THE SCALE ECONOMY ACCOUNT

THE scale economy theory predicts that the country with the largest home markets will export those goods which exhibit the greatest scale economies. Large home markets clearly abet the exploitation of static scale economies; and, insofar as technological progress depends upon accumulated production volume, large home markets may help encourage dynamic scale economies.[1] As a result the big country should enjoy an advantage in producing scale economy goods.

Chemical industry literature often reflects the scale economy theory. For example, F. G. Lamont recently wrote:[2]

> Modern chemical plants cost a lot of money and their size influences their economics. Neglecting the extreme cases, it is customary to consider the cost of the plant and equipment as varying by about the $0 \cdot 6$th power of the capacity. This implies a serious initial disadvantage in the less developed areas since despite their generally large population, demand within the next five to ten years will usually be only a fraction of the accepted size elsewhere.

By implication, less developed areas ought to leave the chemical industry for large, advanced nations and concentrate on industries which exhibit smaller scale economies.* This, of course, is the central theme of the scale economy theory.

Receptive Background. In a free-trade world, however, large nations need not necessarily specialise in scale economy goods. Since trade and production are simultaneous events, small nations might, by anticipating export markets, build huge and economical plants.[3]

As a practical matter, the scale economy theory therefore largely depends upon barriers to free trade. We have already seen

---

* The Egyptian planner might understandably balk at this suggestion. We can well imagine him asking, "Why not establish a plastics industry in Egypt for export to Western Europe, rather than vice versa?"

that transport costs do not substantially hinder synthetic materials commerce.[4] Tariffs and quotas constitute the major barriers. As early as 1916, the United States imposed a 40% tariff on man-made fibres; nine years later, Britain followed suit with a 30% tariff. During the Great Depression, nearly all countries conferred similar protection upon their man-made fibres and plastics industries. And after the Second World War, tariffs were frequently reinforced with quotas. Not only did the dollar-short European countries resort to quantitative controls; the developing nations of Latin America and Asia likewise instituted strong measures to protect infant industry. But the mid-1950s witnessed some relaxation among the industrial nations. Quantitative restrictions were abandoned, and tariffs lowered. Nevertheless, tariffs of 10–20% still prevail in North America and Western Europe, while the developing nations maintain even more stringent barriers.[5]

The impressive scale economies displayed by synthetic materials, coupled with those longstanding trade barriers, should provide a receptive background for the scale economy theory. Diagram 4–1 illustrates this background, insofar as *static* scale economies are concerned. Diagram 4–1 rests on four assumptions. First, we assume that the size of the average synthetic materials plant varies proportionately with the magnitude of national income. If the

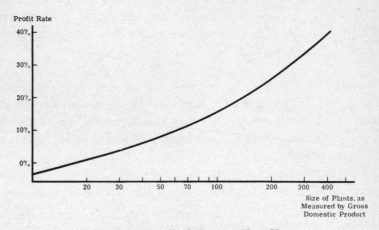

Diagram 4–1.   Profit Rate vs. Plant Size

national income of Germany is $60 billion, and the national income of Italy is $30 billion, then presumably the average German factory is twice as large as the average Italian factory.[6] Second, we suppose that the "plant factor" applied to capital costs is six-tenths for all synthetics, and that the "labour factor" is seven-tenths.[7] Third, we assume that at the United States scale of output, the before-tax profit rate on all synthetic materials is 40%. While this figure exceeds the minimum satisfactory profit rate mentioned in Chapter 3 (25%), it better corresponds to actual conditions.[8] Fourth and last, we assume that the American level of wages and prices prevails in all countries. Thus in Diagram 4 1 the profit rate bears the entire burden of a smaller scale of output. (For the demonstrative purposes of this diagram, we could have assumed alternatively that the same profit rate prevails everywhere, and that the price level reflects changes in the scale of output.)

With these four assumptions, it is a simple matter to find the profit rate on synthetic materials production in countries outside the United States. First, we compute the value added (profits plus wages) for a man-year of output in the United States. For this computation we assume that to produce the average synthetic material in the United States requires $23,000 capital per man.[9] Then we find how much capital and labour would be required to produce the same quantity of output elsewhere.* Wage payments for the requisite labour inputs are deducted from the American value added. The remaining sum, when divided by the capital employed, yields the profit rate.

The actual data underlying Diagram 4-1 is drawn from the year 1960, but the implications of this diagram are quite general.

---

* By assumption, $23,000 capital is utilised in producing an American man-year of output. Also, by assumption, plants in a country with half the gross domestic product of the United States are on the average half as large. The following equation, if solved for K, therefore gives capital employed to produce one-half the American man-year of output in a country whose plants are half as large as those in the United States:

$$\frac{K}{\$23,000} = \left[\frac{1}{2}\right]^{.6}$$

If K is doubled, we then know how much capital is required to produce a full American man-year of output in a country half the size of the United States. A parallel method is applied to find the labour required in such a country. Similar calculations can be made for countries whose gross domestic products are one-third, one fourth, or any other fraction of the United States figure.

If static scale economies are harvested according to home market size, the larger country enjoys a clear production advantage. For while the profit rate is 40% at the American scale of output, it drops to 10% at the Anglo-German scale of output, and barely reaches 5% at the Italian-Japanese scale. The large country can easily offer synthetic materials at a lower price than the small country, yet still earn a greater profit. To be sure, the advantage of the large country would be pared if wage differences were taken into consideration. But it would by no means be eliminated.[10] Moreover, if dynamic scale economies could be taken into consideration the advantages of the large country might well be enhanced—even after allowing for wage differences.

Statistical Analysis. In light of Diagram 4–1 and our general remarks, it is appropriate to test statistically the scale economy theory. Appendix C sets forth the full statistical analysis (the analysis was confined to exports in the 1950s and early 1960s). Since the scale economy theory could not be examined in isolation from the technological gap theory, a more detailed account of the statistical results is given at the close of Chapter 6. However, it may be said here that the size of home markets proved influential in explaining national export shares for plastics and synthetic rubbers exports, but played a small role in explaining export shares for man-made fibres trade.* The partial correlation coefficients between home market size and exports of plastics and synthetic rubbers were 0·722 in 1952, 0·911 in 1957, and 0·345 in 1962. Moreover, in 1962 home market size exercised an indirect effect on exports through its influence upon past production volume (see Appendix C). With regard to man-made fibres trade, the only effect of home market size in those three years was through its influence on past production volume.

The divergent experience between the two groups (plastics and synthetic rubbers on the one hand, man-made fibres on the other) probably stems from different degrees of capital scale economies. Chapter 2 suggested that capital scale economies among plastics

---

* The variable actually analysed was national exports as a percentage of average exports from trading nations. This variable differs from the export share only by a constant multiple; for convenience therefore it is referred to as the export share.

and synthetic rubbers could be described by a "plant factor" of about six-tenths. But for man-made fibres the plant factor is closer to one. The large country does not, therefore, enjoy the same advantage in producing man-made fibres as it does in producing plastics or synthetic rubbers.*

By comparison with its success in explaining absolute trade shares, the size of home markets was easily the best variable for explaining five-year (1952–57 and 1957–62) export share changes for *all* branches of synthetic materials trade. The partial correlation coefficients between home market size changes and export changes exceeded 0·500 in every instance except man-made fibres trade over the 1957–62 period. And the influence of home market size was also expressed indirectly through its effect on past production volume changes.

Probably changes in home market size proved so useful in explaining changes in trade because, as a product becomes older, static advantages assume greater importance. That is, home market sizes play a greater role, while technological disparities and marketing advantages become less crucial.

It may be concluded that the size of home markets, as measured by gross domestic product, exercises considerable influence over the direction of synthetic materials trade. But at the same time it should be remembered that scale economy trade might be much smaller in the absence of tariff barriers protecting home markets.† And even with existing tariff barriers, much synthetic materials commerce depends upon elements of comparative advantage not related to pre-existing home market size. In the remaining chapters, we shall consider those other elements.

REFERENCES

1. Cf. Chapter 1, pp. 21–22, and Chapter 2, pp. 54–57.
2. F. G. Lamont, "Genesis of a Chemical Industry", *New Scientist*, February 14, 1963.

* It should be remembered that labour scale economies are about the same for the two groups of products.
† Moreover, the export share variable may overstate the importance of scale economy trade; see the footnote discussion in Appendix C, p. 121.

3. There is evidence that Switzerland, Sweden, and Belgium have done just that. See the discussion pp. 26–27.

4. Cf. Chapter 1, pp. 14–15, and Appendix A.

5. A fuller discussion of tariff history and the effect of tariffs upon the various nature-of-trade theories is presented in Chapter 3 of my thesis, *Synthetic Materials: A Study in International Trade*, 1963 (Cambridge University Library).

6. Underlying this presumption is the tacit assumption that doubling national income doubles home consumption of the average synthetic material. By and large, this assumption seems reasonable; see Appendix C of my thesis, *op. cit.* However, plants are probably larger in small countries than a proportional relationship would indicate.

7. These figures agree with the findings of Chapter 2, pp. 46–50. It should be recalled that the "plant factor" and the "labour factor" are numbers which relate changes in plant capacity to changes in capital and labour costs. Smaller "factors" imply greater static scale economies.

8. For example, during 1960 American value added per man-year (all employees) in plastics production was $19,000; in synthetic rubbers production $25,000; and in man-made fibres production, $14,700. If $8,000 is subtracted from each of these figures for wage costs, insurance, and miscellaneous items; if a 10% obsolescence charge is entered against profits; and if the resulting figures are compared with the estimated capital employed per man (Table 3–1); then the net before-tax profit was 40% on plastics, 40% on synthetic rubbers, and 35% on man-made fibres. These calculations are based upon U.S. Bureau of Census, *1960 Annual Survey of Manufactures*, 1962. Calculations for earlier years yield similar results.

9. This figure represents a weighted average (weights based on 1960 physical production) of capital-intensities in the three branches of the industry.

10. Cf. pp. 166–170 of my thesis, *op. cit.*

Chapter 5

THE IMITATION LAG

THE factor proportions theory and the scale economy theory have been evaluated. We turn now to the technological gap theory as an explanation of synthetic materials trade.

Posner relates the volume of technological gap trade to the difference between the demand lag and the imitation lag.[1] The demand lag represents the time between the innovating country's first consumption of a new good and the imitating country's first consumption of that good. The imitation lag represents the time between the innovating country's first production and the imitating country's first production of that good. Demand lags are difficult to estimate because trade returns seldom list new products until several years after their commercial introduction. Tentative inquiry suggests, however, that demand lags are ordinarily short, at least among industrial countries. In other words, German plastic fabricators normally accord a new British plastic almost the same reception as do British plastic fabricators. We shall therefore assume that demand lags are typically of unimportant duration. This assumption implies—quite realistically, I think—that imitation lags primarily determine the volume of technological gap trade.

Two terminal dates define imitation lags: the innovation date and the imitation date. Innovation consists of first world production. Imitation consists of first production in any country other than the innovating country. For our purposes, the beginning of small scale commercial production marks first production. Presumably the firm which embarks on commercial production, even on a small scale, pays the utmost attention to reducing costs through improved technology. Inasmuch as technological differences play a vital role in the technological gap theory, innovation and imitation should therefore date from the earliest years of commercial production.

Every country has its own imitation lag for each product. The innovating country's imitation lag is by definition zero years.

Any other country's lag is the number of years from first world production to the date that country undertook manufacture.

Appendix Table C–3 records the dates of first production in each country for each synthetic material.[2] Innovation dates are denoted by an asterisk. Since first production dates are seldom precise down to the month, whenever two countries introduce the same synthetic in the same calendar year, both are classed as innovators.

The preceding paragraphs have broadly defined innovation and imitation dates. Two aspects remain to be considered more closely: financial failure and war. Frequently the initial producer met financial distress before the product achieved commercial success. The patents and equipment were then purchased and successfully exploited by another firm. Under these circumstances, the financially distressed firm is still credited with first production. For according to the presumptions of the technological gap theory, it set in motion the improvement of technology and the consequent acquisition of export markets. As an example, in 1914 the Lustron Co. (formed by the Boston scientist, A. D. Little) began experimenting with cellulose triacetate filaments. In 1916 Lustron made experimental samples, and in 1919 it embarked on very small scale commercial production. But Lustron was never a success, and its assets, patents, and know-how were sold to the Celanese Corporation of America (an affiliate of British Celanese) in 1927. Even so, 1919 is cited as the date of first American production of acetate filament.[3]

War is an abnormal event. Theories of international trade seldom anticipate national hostilities. Certainly the technological gap account does not allow for war. Therefore, in measuring imitation lags, consideration must be taken of the disruptive forces set loose by national hostilities, particularly the Second World War. These disruptive forces are of two types. First, there is the loss of productive facilities through enemy territorial acquisition.* Especially important was the loss of German

---

* Physical destruction of plant might also be included under this category. But physical destruction in Europe and Japan during the Second World War was so varied in extent that it is more suitable to bear in mind that exports should be correspondingly smaller and imports correspondingly larger than imitation lags would indicate during the immediate post-war years.

synthetic rubber plants to the Russian zone after 1945. Many of today's synthetic rubbers were first produced at the famous Schkopau works under the auspices of I.G. Farben between 1933 and 1935. But because these works fell into Russian hands, the inauguration of German production is not dated from the 'thirties. For such a dating would lead to the expectation, in the context of the technological gap theory, of large post-war German synthetic rubber exports.* Exports are clearly impossible when the plant has been seized by a foreign power. Similarly, Germany undertook nylon fibre production in 1939 (one year after America), but again her plants came under Soviet hegemony after the war. Hence the German synthetic rubber and nylon production dates in Appendix Table C–3 refer to the resumption of production at new plant sites after World War II.[4]

The second type of war-induced disruption occurs when priorities halt infant manufacture. In peace time, production develops more or less smoothly, depending upon commercial considerations, from small to large scale levels. But in war time, the introduction of new materials and new techniques is often adjusted to meet the exigencies of the day. And if war priorities dictate the interruption of production, this plainly delays the improvement of technology and prevents the firm from developing capacity to serve home and export markets. Thus it would be inappropriate to specify as an innovation or imitation date the year of first small-scale production if war disrupted the normal sequence. Instead, the date production was resumed after hostilities ended should be cited. For example, the Distiller's Company (Britain) manufactured small amounts of polystyrene between 1939 and 1943, but then stopped production in view of war needs. Manufacture was not resumed until 1950. Hence 1950 is, for our purposes, the date of first polystyrene production in Britain.

These remarks cover most of the important criteria used in selecting innovation and imitation dates. The remaining difficulties usually arose from conflicting historical statements. Such

* There was no pre-war trade in synthetic rubber, or, for that matter, in any other product subjected to the same measure of war-induced disruption.

conflicts were resolved by writing the interested firms and then relying upon the most plausible source.

Measuring Aggregate Imitation Lags. The imitation lag for a particular product and country is the time from innovation (first world production) to that country's imitation. Germany discovered and first produced galalith in 1899. Britain first produced this plastic in 1912, and America in 1919. Germany's imitation lag for galalith was zero years: by definition the innovator's imitation lag is always nil. Britain's imitation lag for galalith was 13 years. America's lag was 20 years. The imitation lag for an individual product is given by simple subtraction.

To a certain extent the technological gap theory might be tested on an individual product basis by comparing trade flows with national imitation lags. But an aggregative evaluation of the theory is clearly desirable. One simply cannot sift and weigh all the individual examples of technological gap trade which might occur among fifty synthetic materials and at least a dozen major countries. An aggregate analysis, however, requires some method of adding together imitation lags for different products. Suppose Britain had a 7-year lag in celluloid manufacture, a 13-year lag in galalith production, and a nil lag in polyethylene production. Should we simply average these three lags so that Britain's "aggregate imitation lag" for the three plastics taken as a whole is 6·67 years $(7+13+0=20; 20/3=6·67)$? A simple average is surely wrong if we wish to relate the aggregate imitation lag to the trade conditions of the day. The fact that Britain produced a celluloid in 1877, 7 years after America, and galalith in 1912, 13 years after Germany, makes very little difference to plastics trade in 1962. For by comparison with polyethylene, celluloid and galalith are now produced and exported in insignificant quantities. Twenty-five years ago the position was reversed: in 1937, polyethylene was an important infant.

In order that "aggregate imitation lags" relate to the trade conditions of the day, the imitation lag for each product is weighted by that product's share of current world exports.* The weighted imitation lags are then added together to give an aggregate imitation lag for the country. For example, suppose that in 1962 polyethylene accounted for 80% of world plastics exports, and that galalith and celluloid each made up 10%. Britain's aggregate imitation lag would then be 2·00 years (10% × 7 + 10% × 13 + 80% × 0 = 2·00).† A minor difficulty arises in calculating aggregate imitation lags when a country does not yet produce some synthetic material. In 1930 Canada had not yet produced galalith. What then was to be the imitation lag for galalith in calculating Canada's 1930 aggregate plastics imitation lag? The Canadian galalith imitation lag in 1930 should be the time between first world production of galalith (1899, in Germany) and 1930, or 31 years. With a 31-year galalith imitation lag in 1930, we should automatically expect Canadian galalith imports to account for her entire domestic consumption and her exports to be nil, because 31 years was the "maximum imitation lag" for galalith in 1930. Countries which do not yet produce certain goods are thus assigned the "maximum imitation lag" for those goods. When a country's imitation lag approaches the maximum, her trade must inevitably conform to the predictions of the technological gap account; a country which does not manufacture a good must import all her domestic requirements, and cannot be expected to have any exports.

An important question remains: should individual imitation lags be weighted by value or tonnage figures in computing the aggregate imitation lag? Expediency dictates tonnage figures:

* Weighting by world exports rather than world production may in some instances overstate a nation's imitative prowess. For example, as an explanation of British imports it might be terribly important that Britain had failed to manufacture a big-volume plastic in which all other nations were self-sufficient. This plastic would carry a small weight in world trade (by virtue of national self-sufficiency), and thus the British aggregate lag would not be much affected. But still Britain might pay a large import bill to satisfy home consumption. If common, such situations would obviously call for production weights rather than trade weights in measuring aggregate imitation lags. However, these situations occur infrequently; while for analysing exports (the focus of our statistical efforts) production weights exaggerate the importance of having been an early producer of older goods—goods which are still consumed in large quantity, but are no longer traded in substantial volume.

† Chapter 1 suggested that a 7-year imitation lag incurred on a product now 50 years old is less important than a 7-year lag incurred on a product now 10 years old. While this suggestion has considerable merit, there is no ready method of taking it into account. However, the relative decline of older products automatically reduces the importance of their lags, since such lags are accorded a smaller weight.

value figures are simply not available. Appendix Table C–4 presents the tonnage weights employed in computing aggregate imitation lags for various years.

Although the data left no alternative, value weights admittedly might have been preferable to tonnage weights. Broadly speaking, two discernible biases are introduced by using tonnage rather than value weights, and by talking about trade in tonnage rather than value terms. First, man-made fibres are grossly understated. Whereas plastics and synthetic rubbers have typically sold for $700–$800 per metric ton, man-made fibres have usually commanded twice that price. Since man-made fibres represent an older group, in which trade is more influenced by wage rates, one's impression of total synthetic materials therefore underestimates the role of wage rates.[5] Second, new products are understated. The normal synthetic material falls in price as it grows older. And the imitation lag primarily influences trade in younger products. On this count, the regression analyses underestimate the importance of imitation lags. To a certain extent these two biases counteract each other; and it would be difficult to say on balance which is stronger.

Appendix Table C–5, based on Tables C–3 and C–4, gives aggregate imitation lags for each group of synthetic materials, for plastics and synthetic rubbers taken together, and for synthetic materials as a whole. It also presents maximum aggregate imitation lags. Diagram 5–1 charts the paths of aggregate imitation lags (all synthetics) for a number of countries from 1910 to 1960, as well as the maximum lag. Over this 50-year span, many nations have substantially decreased their lags. Italy, Japan, and Canada have been outstanding in this regard.*

The general shortening of imitation lags reflects the spread of industry predicted by the technological gap theory. A country may decrease its lag in two ways. First, it may undertake production of materials which it has not hitherto manufactured. (In the extreme case it may introduce altogether new materials.) Even if a country begins making a material of declining import-

---

* It is worth mentioning that the rapid reduction in Canada's aggregate lag has been materially assisted by Anglo-American ownership of almost the entire Canadian plastics and man-made fibres industries. In this respect, Canada presents an interesting contrast to Sweden, which has very few foreign interests in her chemical industry.

ance, that will contribute to a shorter lag. But obviously a nation will do better by making materials of growing importance. The second method, then, of decreasing the imitation lag is by manufacturing those materials destined for greater prominence in future years. Newer materials usually enjoy the greatest growth and thus offer the best selection. As evidence of this rule, the maximum aggregate imitation lag (all synthetics) has remained remarkably constant at about 30 years during the past half-century. The maximum aggregate imitation lag is simply the weighted age of current exports (dating each product from the year of innovation).[6] In other words, during the past half-century, a synthetic material was likely to be exported in greatest quantity, relative to other synthetics, when it was about 30 years

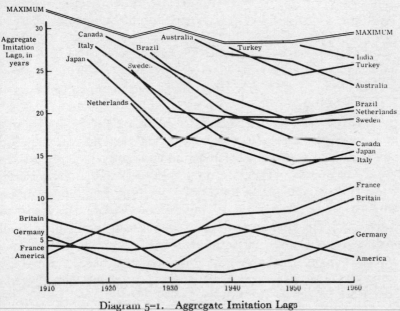

Diagram 5–1. Aggregate Imitation Lags
Source: Appendix Table C–5.

old. After that, the material's relative importance (and consequently its weight in calculating imitation lags) declined. Therefore, materials younger than 30 years have historically offered the best prospects.[7] The best way for a nation to have decreased its plastics imitation lag in 1962 was to have had the foresight to undertake polyvinyl chloride, polystyrene, and polyethylene production in the 1930s or early 1940s. Some of the countries which noticeably shortened their lags did just that.*

Although Diagram 5–1 attests to the spread of synthetic materials manufacturing, it also shows that leaders remain leaders. Either by innovating the new products themselves, or by imitating new products made elsewhere, the advanced countries extend their leadership from one decade to the next. This sequence is not inevitable. An underdeveloped country may, with some effort, break into the ranks of leading nations, while a leader may falter and slip behind. But there are strong forces maintaining the status quo.

Innovation and Imitation. To appreciate the forces preserving the status quo, it may be useful to review the innovating and imitating process.

Innovation obviously requires scientific sophistication and a good command of engineering technology. America, Germany, Britain, France, and Italy have discovered almost all of today's synthetic materials. Yet it is not true that the locus of "basic" research necessarily determines the locus of innovation.[8] Time and time again the basic research underlying the synthesis of a new material has taken place in one country and actual production started in another. Cellulose nitrate, for example, was explored by C. F. Schoenbein, a Swiss-German, in 1845, and by A. Parkes, an Englishman, from 1855 to 1865. But it was J. W. Hyatt, an American, who produced the first commercial celluloid in 1870. Likewise, three famous British scientists, C. F. Cross, E. J. Bevan, and C. H. Stearn, first prepared viscose solutions and experimented with their film and fibre properties. But La Cellophane, a French firm working under the direction of J. E. Brandenberger, first produced cellophane film in 1917. To cite one more example, F. S. Kipping, a Briton, devoted his entire academic life (1899–1944) to the study of silicone compounds. Silicone compounds

---

* This is not to imply that a shorter aggregate imitation lag is a meaningful goal in itself. It is meaningful primarily in the context of improving the nation's balance of payments. And even if a country wishes to improve its balance of payments, there are ways of doing so which will not be reflected in a shorter imitation lag: e.g., further import substitution of a good already produced at home.

were also examined in France and Russia during the 1930s. Yet the United States produced the first silicone plastics and rubbers during the Second World War. Thus, a flourishing scientific community, which freely publishes its findings, typically makes a general contribution to the innovation of new synthetic materials, rather than a specific contribution to its own nation's prowess.

Probably, therefore, the national location of innovation is more closely tied to the research carried on *within* industrial firms than to national scientific effort as a whole. Du Pont's nylon and acetal discoveries suggest that a substantial quantum of research can be achieved within the company framework. The same conclusion emerges from studying I.C.I.'s polyethylene and Montecatini's polypropylene discoveries. And in each case the research was communicated to the scientific world only *after* key patents had been filed and development work commenced.* But whether overall research or industry research provides the key to innovation, it seems certain that the developed nations of Europe and North America enjoy a firm hold on the discovery of new materials.†

The rapidity with which imitation takes place is also linked to the general state of development.‡ And imitation dates exert greater force in determining national lags than innovation dates. Neither the United States nor Germany would have small aggregate imitation lags but for rapid imitation. The main

* During the nineteenth century, most fundamental scientific research was undertaken either by men of independent means or through the universities. Results were rapidly communicated to interested parties everywhere. Nineteenth-century research was open in character: scientific endeavour was not yet firmly linked with industrial profits. Today, private industry performs most non-military research. Universities and research institutions sponsor a rather smaller proportion, while wealthy individuals have almost retired from the scene. Accordingly a large proportion of current research receives only cryptic reporting in the patent literature.

† As this book was going to print, the author had an opportunity to read a paper by R. Vernon, Harvard University, titled "International Investment in the Trade Cycle". Professor Vernon makes the interesting suggestion that the locus of innovation depends very much on the locus of a receptive market. New products which are geared to high per capita income levels (such as nylon), or which offer substantial labour savings (such as fork-lift trucks) are thus likely to be first introduced in high-income, high-labour-cost markets.

‡ My doctoral dissertation contended that labour-intensive goods should be imitated more rapidly than capital-intensive goods, considering the factor price patterns in potential innovating and imitating nations. Scant empirical evidence was found for this proposition however. Vernon, in the paper just mentioned, has suggested that standardisation may be the key to imitation. The more rapidly the product or process is standardised, the more rapidly it will be imitated by foreign nations.

difference between Japan and Brazil, neither of which has innovated any important synthetic materials, is that Japan has imitated much more quickly.

It might appear obvious that advanced nations should be faster imitators than their neighbours. Chapter 1 suggested this very theme. But the present discussion illustrates how the *mechanics* of imitation favour more advanced nations. It will facilitate the discussion to distinguish three "imitating routes": independent research, licensing, and foreign subsidiaries.

The independent research "route" implies that the imitating firm develops the material independently. The task of the independent research imitator varies enormously from case to case. At one extreme, two sophisticated firms may experiment with a new material at about the same time. In these instances, the imitator probably expends as much scientific effort as the innovator. For example, Sir James Swinburne filed a British patent on phenol formaldehyde only one day after Dr. Leo Baekeland filed an American patent. Baekeland's firm began producing phenol formaldehyde in 1909, and Swinburne's firm in 1910. Likewise, Dynamit AG (Germany) innovated polystyrene in 1930, and Naugatuck Chemical (United States) independently produced polystyrene in 1933. Italy and Germany manufactured linear polyethylene by the Ziegler process in 1954 and 1955 respectively, while America began producing this plastic in 1956 by the somewhat different Phillips process. Such instances of simultaneous experimentation necessarily involve the most advanced countries, where sophisticated chemical firms continually stay abreast of the latest developments.

Another variation of independent research imitation occurs when an aversion to paying royalties, or the difficulty of acquiring a licence, spurs the imitator to develop his own manufacturing process or variation of the new material. Such imitators typically begin research after the product is on the market, and therefore know approximately the object of investigation. Occasionally the imitator further eases his scientific (if not his legal) task by purchasing key personnel from an innovating firm. For instance, the Belgian cellophane producer SIDAC was established with the assistance of the chief engineer from La Cellophane, who "absconded with blueprints and complete information as to La Cellophane's secret process for cellophane manufacture".[9] This type of independent research imitation clearly demands less scientific brilliance than does innovation. Still, it is usually restricted to the more advanced nations. For even when the "research" consists more of sharp practice than scientific endeavour, it requires a high degree of technical sophistication to put the abstract knowledge to commercial use.

The least scientifically taxing cases of independent research imitation arise when an imitating firm begins production after technology becomes an open secret and key patents have expired. Countries with long imitation lags frequently practise this kind of imitation. After a material passes a certain age—perhaps 20 or 30 years—fairly detailed production descriptions have usually been published. Moreover, when a material is that old, technicians are easily found who can assist in designing and operating a plant. The imitation of galalith in the United States (1919) and Holland (1920); of celluloid in Switzerland (1923); of phenol formaldehyde in Argentina (1947) and India (1948); and of nitrocellulose rayon in Brazil (1936), all represent this type of independent research imitation. The "packaged plant", a speciality of some European and American chemical engineering firms, represents the epitome of this variety of imitation.[10] Packaged plants require an absolute minimum of preliminary scientific or technical effort on the part of local management. Hence, they have become an important vehicle for developing the synthetic materials industry in less advanced regions. But, of course, packaged plants are usually available for only the older and more familiar products.

To sum up: if a country depends upon independent research, then the more advanced the country, the more likely it will possess the requisite scientific and technical talent for early imitation. Less advanced countries imitate via independent research primarily when materials are older, and the effort commensurately less demanding.

Licensing by a foreign producer furnishes the second "imitating route". Aside from the inducement of royalties, there are certain special incentives which stimulate the flow of licences between the major North Atlantic countries. The well-worn licensing paths within and between Europe and America are easily the most significant feature of the licensing "route". The rapid flow of licences between Germany, Britain, France, and America has substantially buttressed the synthetic materials leadership of these countries, and has helped ensure short lags. Three special incentives predispose each leading country to license production of new materials in the other leading countries before considering applicants from elsewhere in the world.

First, there is the matter of reciprocity. If I.C.I. licenses Du Pont on a newly discovered plastic, then Du Pont may later license I.C.I. on a new fibre. The reciprocity incentive generally stimulates the flow of licences between leading producers in the major countries. Pechiney supports I.C.I.; I.C.I. supports BASF; BASF supports Du Pont; and Du Pont supports Courtaulds. Licensing reciprocity requires no prior written agreement. It is based on the mutual realisation that leading producers have the best research facilities and are most likely to discover new materials.

Second, innovators often grant licences to leading producers elsewhere simply to forestall them from pursuing the independent research route to imitation. As one trade journal remarked:[11]

> . . . the threat of its own research facilities is often the only weapon whereby one company may persuade another that there is more to gain by granting licences than by trying to maintain exclusivity.

The third incentive for cross-licensing between leading firms in advanced countries likewise stems from their higher level of technical skill. If Du Pont develops a new product, it can teach I.C.I. or Bayer the manufacturing process with minimal effort. In a sense, these firms speak the same language. But it would take Du Pont much longer, and it would require more valuable manpower, to impart adequate technical know-how to an African, Asian, or Latin American firm.*

Foreign subsidiaries comprise the last "imitating route" which

---

* The story is told about an American chemical firm which established a fairly basic chemical plant in the Iberian peninsula. It started by teaching the local "chemical engineers" the centigrade scale.

we have distinguished. This route embraces instances where a foreign producer of the synthetic owns or acquires a capital interest in the imitating firm. Many materials, to be sure, were first produced in America, Britain, Germany, and France by foreign subsidiaries. But the foreign subsidiary route is peculiarly suited to the less advanced countries. If a sophisticated chemical firm must furnish extensive technical assistance before a new product can be manufactured in a less developed region, then it might just as well establish a foreign subsidiary and reap the profits of its expertise. I.C.I., for example, introduced polyethylene to India via its subsidiary, Alkali and Chemical Corp., and polyvinyl chloride to Brazil via ELCLORO. The Celanese Corp. of America introduced acetate filament and staple, and several other fibres, to Mexico via Celanese Mexicana. Dow Chemical and Monsanto Chemical have spread the manufacture through subsidiaries. And Hoechst initiated polyvinyl acetate production in South Africa through Mowolith, and in Spain through Electro-Quimica de Flix.

Foreign subsidiaries may offer the best hope for less advanced nations to shorten their imitation lags. Once a leading chemical firm has established a foreign subsidiary in an underdeveloped country, the obstacles to introducing new synthetics are minimized. But subsidiaries are never likely to shorten aggregate imitation lags below the length prevailing in advanced countries. For the parent firm will almost always produce the new material at home and export it for some time before undertaking production abroad.

Thus, to a very large extent, national imitation lag differences are grounded in the structure of the whole economy. This is illustrated by Diagram 5-2 which graphs 1957 aggregate imitation lags against 1957 per capita production of manufactures for various countries. New products spread very much like new fashions: from highly developed centres to somewhat less developed regions, then to remote areas. As parallel examples we may cite the "twist", a dance that was popular a few years ago, and nylon fibre. Boston's society was "twisting" in June 1961. By December 1961 fashionable Parisian and London circles were learning the dance. But Athenians did no twisting until April 1962; and

Yugoslavia's Macedonians depended on 1962's summer tourists to teach them to twist. In much the same manner, America produced nylon fibre in 1938, and both Britain and France were manufacturing nylon in 1941. However, Greece did not manufacture nylon until 1961; and in Yugoslavia, this fibre is still "under consideration".

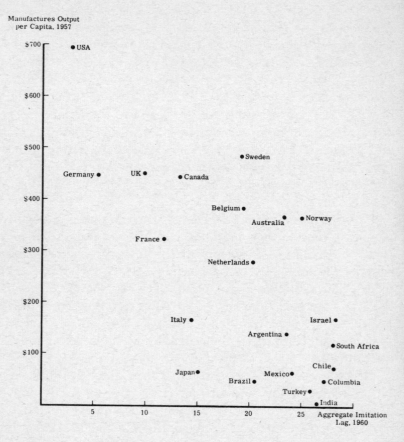

Diagram 5–2. Imitation Lags and Per Capita Output of Manufactures
Sources: A. Maizels, *Industrial Growth and World Trade*, 1963, Table E–4; Appendix Table C–5.

REFERENCES

1. M. V. Posner, "International Trade and Technical Change", *Oxford Economic Papers*, October 1961.

2. For most synthetics, Appendix Table C–3 records the date of whichever sub-form was first manufactured in the country concerned. But the Table often lists both sub-forms of man-made fibres—filament and staple—since they differ substantially with respect to production processes and markets.

3. Cf. *Textile Organon*, "Base Book", January 1958.

4. The styrene, nitrile, and butyl synthetic rubber dates asterisked in Appendix Table C–3 as "innovation" dates do not, therefore, represent the true first world production.

5. No regression analysis is performed on total synthetic materials; rather, plastics and synthetic rubbers are analysed as one group, and man-made fibres as another (see Appendix C).

6. This is true because the weighted age of current exports would be calculated just as was the maximum aggregate imitation lag: each product would be weighted according to its share of current exports, and each product's age would be measured as the number of years from innovation to the present.

7. The composition of exports is younger than the overall composition of production. This point is discussed in Chapter 6 in connection with the technological gap theory.

8. Cf. J. L. Enos, "Invention and Innovation in the Petroleum Refining Industry", Table 2, in Universities-National Bureau Committee for Economic Research, *The Rate and Direction of Inventive Activity*, 1962.

9. United States vs. Du Pont, *118 Federal Supplement 41*, 1954, Finding 615.

10. The packaged plant was pioneered by Von Kohorn Co. (Germany) which supplied machinery and technical assistance for establishing the viscose rayon industry in Czechoslovakia (1919), Greece (1923), Turkey (1935), Rumania (1937), Peru (1946), and Egypt (1948). A. H. Hard, *The Rayon Year Book*, 1948.

11. *European Chemical News*, April 27, 1962.

Chapter 6

THE TECHNOLOGICAL GAP ACCOUNT

LET us review the idealised technological gap trade pattern. The innovating country initially exports large quantities of the new product. Later, when the imitating country undertakes manufacture, the innovator's exports diminish. The same pattern applies to trade between early and late imitators: the early imitator exports to the late imitator until the latter country erects its own facilities and develops comparable technology.

What is the impact of wage differences upon this pattern? We know that high-wage countries normally innovate new products. Consequently "low-wage trade" should eventually supplant "technological gap trade". For presumably at some point the low-wage country will develop sufficient know-how and facilities that its labour advantage will overcome the high-wage nation's lead in improving technology and harvesting static scale economies. And at that point, the low-wage nation should reverse the flow of trade and begin exporting to the high-wage nation.

The technological gap account thus embodies two successive kinds of commerce: technological gap trade followed by low-wage trade. We shall first examine the evidence for low-wage trade.

Low-Wage Trade. Low-wage trade may be identified in two different ways. One method is to cite as low-wage trade that portion of total export variance explained by the wage variable in a multiple regression analysis. Another method is to classify trade returns as to origin and destination, and thereby derive a rough and ready estimation of the volume of low-wage trade. Here we shall pursue the second' approach. Later in the chapter, however, the results of the regression analysis will be discussed. To distinguish low-wage trade from the remainder of synthetic materials commerce, three simplifying rules may be followed. First, all United States and Canadian imports from third countries can be designated low-wage trade. Second, Japanese, Italian,

Austrian, and Spanish exports to other European countries or Oceania can be designated low-wage trade. And third, all exports from Latin America, Asia (except Japan), and Africa can be similarly categorized, if sent to Europe, Oceania, or Japan.

Theory predicts that as a product passes from youth to maturity, low-wage exports should claim a larger and larger fraction of trade. The behaviour of commodity groups substantiates this prediction. Within a commodity group, new products continuously supplant older products; hence the age of a commodity group is measured as the weighted age of the constituent products. The maximum aggregate imitation lag provides this measure.* Diagram 6–1 graphs maximum lags for various groups at different times against the proportion of low-wage trade in those groups.

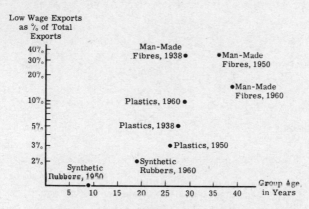

Diagram 6–1. Low-Wage Exports vs. Group Age

While no exact relationship exists between the two variables, it does appear that low-wage trade has greater importance in an older group.

Italy, Japan, and Austria have been the leading exporters of low-wage goods. But not all synthetic materials exports from these nations fall into the classification of low-wage trade. A considerable portion of Italian, Japanese, and Austrian exports are in fact sent to less developed countries (with correspondingly lower wages) such as India, Brazil, Libya, Ceylon, Hong Kong, Formosa,

* The maximum aggregate imitation lag is simply the average age of all products (dating each product from the year of innovation), with each age weighted by the importance of the product in current exports.

and Egypt. For example, about 48% of Japanese plastics exports in 1960 were sent to countries with lower wages than Japan. Likewise, over 60% of Italian synthetic rubber exports in 1960 went to less developed regions, rather than to the advanced nations of Europe and North America.[1] Because of tariff barriers and competition from established producers, an industrializing nation may find export markets easier in nations three steps behind than in nations three steps ahead.

In any case, a new producing nation typically sends low-wage exports to nations which preceded her in manufacturing the goods, and sends exports based on technological advantages to nations which have not yet erected their own plants. Table 6–1 illustrates

Table 6–1. Low-Wage Trade in Man-Made Fibres

	1960 Exports	1960 Imports
United States	0%	100%
Germany	12%	52%
Italy	24%	12%
Japan	12%	0%

Source: Official trade statistics. Based on weight, not value.

this hierarchy of trade with man-made fibres experience. This table distinguishes low-wage imports and exports from four leading nations: the United States, Germany, Italy, and Japan. Clearly, no American exports are low-wage trade, but all American man-made fibre imports belong to that category. Moving down the wage scale, a greater dependence on low-wage exports and a lesser reliance on low-wage imports becomes evident. However, only 12% of Japanese man-made fibre exports in 1960 were low-wage trade (and the figure was only slightly higher before World War II). Japanese experience again suggests that even when a country has a clear wage advantage *vis-à-vis* advanced nations, technological gap exports may still offer more promise than low wage exports.

Granting the existence of low-wage trade, it still appears that such commerce has never been prominent among synthetic materials. At its peak, low-wage trade comprised about 35% of man-made fibres exports—just before the Second World War and again in 1950. It has always been smaller among plastics and synthetic rubbers. Perhaps a slower rate of synthetic materials innovation would allow low-wage trade to assume greater importance. But heretofore, low-wage trade has evidently played a small role.

It should be noted that the multiple regression analysis (presented later) accords even a smaller role to low-wage trade than the foregoing analysis. The wage variable did not help explain plastics and synthetic rubbers trade, and it was statistically significant for explaining man-made fibre exports only in 1962.[2]

Now let us turn to the evidence for technological gap trade. The evidence is divided into three categories. First, individual examples of such trade are discussed. Next, the predicted relationships between product age and trade volume are examined. Last, the statistical analysis introduced in Chapter 4 is reviewed.

Examples of Trade History. Posner explicitly formulated the concept of technological gap trade. However, many writers have commented on individual instances of technological gap trade, without stressing its wider significance. For example, D. C. Hague wrote in 1957:[3]

> One feature of the pre-war growth of viscose rayon staple fibre output was that much of the increasing output went to North America. "The British rayon industry was much quicker than its American counterpart to realize the importance of rayon staple. British staple was much sought after in the United States."* In 1938, out of a total output of 32·4 million lb. of staple fibre, 11·7 million lb. was exported to the United States, despite the fact that total exports were only 14·2 million lb. In 1939, exports to America rose to 28 million lb., out of total exports of 32·4 million lb. and a total output of 57·6 million lb.

* *Times Review of Industry*, August 1951, p. 60.

It may be useful, therefore, to present some examples of technological gap trade.

The first example concerns German galalith experience. Casein, a substance which comes from milk, serves as the primary raw material for galalith. Galalith was discovered and first marketed by International Galalith Gesellschaft Hoff & Co. at the turn of the century (during its initial years, this firm operated under another name). Since casein was largely produced in France and Argentina, the industry might more logically, from the raw material viewpoint, have been located in one of those two countries. But Germany had the technology. To be sure, France undertook production a few years later, but for a long time German galalith was known for its superior quality. Britain first manufactured galalith in 1912; other European nations did not start until after the First World War, and then usually with the assistance of German emigrants. Under these circumstances, International Galalith retained its lead during the 1920s and, as Diagram 6–2 shows, German galalith exports were sizeable. Moreover, the export market contributed substantially to German exploitation of static scale economies, for throughout the 1920s it absorbed between 50% and 90% of German galalith output.

German galalith imports were also growing during the 1920s, largely supplied by Estonia and Britain. Estonian galalith exports, primarily based on lower wage rates, represented the inevitable sequence to technological gap trade. The same cannot be said of British exports. Anglo-German galalith trade (Germany was also sending galalith to Britain) was an exchange between countries with approximately equal technology and wage rates. If galalith were a perfectly homogeneous commodity then, according to Posner's model, there should have been no trade once Britain had achieved technological parity. But firms in each country developed minor specialties, which they then exported to the other country. Besides, negligible transport costs permitted some Anglo-German cross-hauling of equivalent galalith grades, just as within a single country firms invade each other's "home territory".

German galalith exports dropped considerably during the 1930s. By this time the important consuming nations had established their own plants, few aspects of galalith technology remained secret (detailed books had been published on the subject), and new plastics were offering substantial competition (phenol formaldehyde, urea formaldehyde). Moreover, many nations were busily erecting tariff barriers. Germany herself imposed a fairly high galalith tariff in 1933, and, as Diagram 6–2 shows, her imports also declined during this period.

The second example shows the relationship between technological gap trade and low-wage trade. Italian celluloid commerce —Diagram 6–3—provides a classic instance of low-wage exports

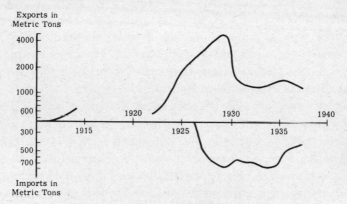

Diagram 6–2.   German Galalith Trade

Sources: A. P. Koch, *Die Deutsche Kunstwerkstoffindustrie*, 1939; J. Delorme, *Le Commerce des Matières Plastiques dans le Monde*, 1956.

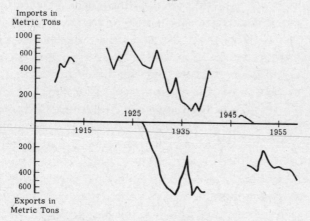

Diagram 6–3.   Italian Celluloid Trade

Sources: J. Delorme, *Le Commerce des Matières Plastiques dans le Monde*, 1956; official trade statistics.

supplanting technological gap imports. Before 1924 Italy produced no celluloid, despite a well developed fabricating industry located in Piacenza and Brescia which made, and indeed exported, celluloid combs, buttons, and knife handles from imported block celluloid. Most of the imported celluloid came from Britain, France and Germany—countries with decidedly higher wages than Italy. But in 1924 Du Pont collaborated with a local Italian firm, M. Pompeo Mazzucchelli, to establish the Societa Italiana della Celluloid. The venture was quite profitable, owing to low Italian wage rates and the ready local market. Shortly, other Italian celluloid firms began production. Italy soon replaced her technological gap imports of celluloid with domestically produced material, and even began exporting to her former suppliers, as Diagram 6–3 shows. Since the Second World War, newer plastics have limited Italy's low-wage celluloid exports.

Many synthetics developed during the 1930s are still too young for either home production in the less advanced regions or low-wage exports to have supplanted exports from Western Europe or North America. Yet in several cases involving newer products, the advanced nation clearly owes her exports to early manufacture and attendant technological superiority, rather than to any raw material or factor cost advantage. The history of high pressure polyethylene is illustrative.

High pressure polyethylene was introduced by Britain in 1937 and America undertook production in 1941. At the close of the Second World War, both countries had sizeable facilities and probably enjoyed comparable technology. Owing to brisk civilian demand, the United States did not offer any polyethylene to export markets until the early 1950s. Diagram 6–4 shows the course of American shipments since that time. Exports have grown immensely, and they now exceed 100,000 metric tons annually. By all indications, British exports have been equally buoyant.[4]

Anglo-American polyethylene exports stem primarily from the relatively long imitation lags of other countries. Germany was manufacturing polyethylene when the Second World War ended, but for a long while her technology was probably not equivalent to Anglo-American practice. And at least until the early 1950s,

German chemical firms were hampered by the sheer volume of war destruction. Italy began producing polyethylene in 1952, France and Japan not until 1954. Most other countries waited until the late 1950s or the early 1960s before undertaking production.

By the time these other countries did begin production, both America and Britain had already harvested enormous static scale

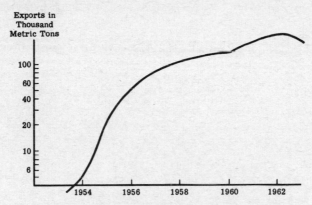

Diagram 6–4.   American High Pressure Polyethylene Exports
Source: Official trade statistics.

economies. This harvest was materially assisted by foreign sales: in 1960, exports absorbed almost a third of total United States production, and the British fraction was doubtless higher. Anglo-American producers developed home per capita consumption ahead of foreign practice, which also encouraged static scale economy exploitation. Besides, polyethylene process speeds—dynamic scale economies—achieved in these countries were almost certainly greater than the process speeds achieved by newcomers.

To be sure, America has long enjoyed an ample petroleum supply. But so have other countries in the Western hemisphere, not to mention the Middle East and Asia. And throughout, America has been handicapped by decidedly higher wage rates. Britain, on the other hand, has not even enjoyed the luxury of home-produced petroleum. It therefore seems clear that both countries have relied more upon their production lead than upon pre-existing factor endowments to provide a comparative advantage in polyethylene trade. If the technological gap account is correct, then Anglo-American polyethylene exports should diminish during the next decade. Indeed, American exports in 1963 fell by 30,000 metric tons over the 1962 figure, even though world consumption continued its rapid rise.[5] Eventually, if America relaxes her high tariff barriers, her exports may be partly supplanted by low-wage imports.

Japanese polyvinyl chloride trade illustrates how an imitating nation may send low-wage exports to advanced regions and

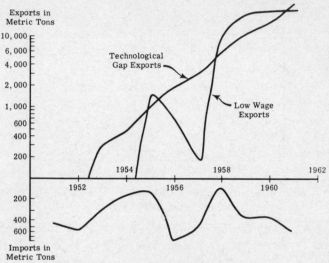

Diagram 6–5. Japanese Polyvinyl Chloride Exports
Source: Official trade statistics.

technological gap exports to less developed areas. Japan produced some polyvinyl chloride during the Second World War, but output remained on a small scale until 1949. At that time the Japanese government deliberately encouraged polyvinyl chloride, and output expanded rapidly during the 1950s. Diagram 6–5 records Japanese polyvinyl chloride trade history. Imports, all consisting of technological gap trade from Western Europe and North America, have remained small. But exports have grown rapidly. The technological gap component of exports comprises sales to Korea, Formosa, Burma, India, Brazil, Nigeria, and similar nations. These countries pay lower industrial wages than Japan, and Japanese exports are primarily predicated on technological superiority. The low-wage component of exports, on the other hand, comprises sales to Western Europe, North America, and Oceania. This segment of polyvinyl chloride trade mainly rests on lower labour costs rather than superior technology.

Interestingly enough, Japanese technological gap exports of polyvinyl chloride have expanded far more regularly than her low-wage exports of this plastic. Underdeveloped areas usually offer no local competition, and Japanese exports have correspondingly grown with demand. By contrast, Japanese exports to the advanced nations have met considerable local resistance. As a result, these exports have been rather erratic.

The foregoing examples represent a few of the many slices of trade history which might be interpreted within the technological gap framework. Let us now attempt to supplement this type of analysis with a more aggregative evaluation of the theory.

Product Age and Trade Volume. Posner's basic theme that, with time, technology spreads from very developed centres to less developed regions suggests the corollary that advanced nations mainly export newer synthetic materials. For as a synthetic passes from youth to old age, more countries undertake manufacture, and exports from the innovating centres correspondingly decline.

This corollary cannot be tested simply by looking at the absolute volume of advanced nations' exports. Production of some old synthetics greatly exceed production of newer ones; in such circumstances, exports of the older goods are naturally larger in absolute terms. It is more appropriate to express the corollary in relative terms: advanced nations should export a bigger *fraction* of their production of new synthetics than of old synthetics. The United States is the only advanced nation which publishes sufficiently detailed production and trade statistics to test this corollary with any precision.

Diagram 6–6 compares the fraction of American output exported in 1960 with the date of first manufacture of the product in question. This diagram includes both plastics and synthetic rubbers, since these two groups belong to roughly the same "class", in terms of processes and capital-intensities. Occasionally the statistics necessitated coupling two or more products together. In that case, the first American production date is a weighted average of the first production dates of the various products. The weights are determined in the same manner as those used in calculating aggregate imitation lags: they are based on an estimate of each product's contribution to current exports.

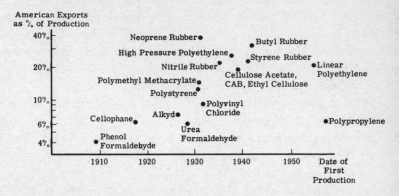

Diagram 6–6. American Plastics and Synthetic Rubber Exports

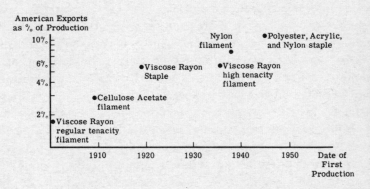

Diagram 6–7. American Man-Made Fibres Exports

Diagram 6–6 shows that the United States exhibits a pronounced tendency to specialise in her newer plastics and synthetic rubbers. In fact, the tendency is so strong that a logarithmic relationship apparently best suits the data. But there are three products which conspicuously deviate from the others. The first is neoprene, a special purpose synthetic rubber devised by Du Pont in 1931.

Neoprene exports seem unduly large in relation to the age of this rubber. The reason is that the spread of neoprene production to other countries has been somewhat retarded. Du Pont authorised no foreign production before licensing Bayer in 1956.* Two reasons probably account for the slow spread of production: the special purpose nature of neoprene, and Du Pont's reluctance to encourage foreign production before markets had developed sufficiently.

The other two products which deviate conspicuously are linear polyethylene and polypropylene. These very new plastics were exported in relatively small quantities during 1960. Home demand was so brisk that producers had little output to spare for foreign markets. It is probably fair to conclude that when a synthetic material is very young, exports may take only a small fraction of output. In the present example, this phenomenon results from brisk home demand; but exports might also be retarded by a lack of foreign enthusiasm (Posner's demand lag). Although exports should ultimately rise, in 1963 United States linear polyethylene exports still amounted to only 8% of output.[6]

Diagram 6-7 plots American man-made fibre exports against first American production dates. Clearly, America specialises in exporting the newer nylon, polyester, and acrylic fibres and the newer forms of viscose rayon, rather than the older man-made fibres. The discovery and introduction of many of these new fibres has, in fact, transformed America into a major man-made fibre exporter since 1938. Still, the United States does not export nearly such a large percentage of her man-made fibres output as her plastics or synthetic rubbers output, even for products of the same vintage. The reason perhaps is that man-made fibres are more labour-intensive than the other two groups of synthetic materials.[7]

With sufficient aggregation, the age composition of trade may be examined from a world viewpoint. We have gathered data on five different groups of synthetic materials: cellulosic and thermo-set plastics, thermoplastic plastics, synthetic rubbers, man-made filaments, and man-made staple. Plastics and man-made fibres

---

* A Du Pont subsidiary began production in Britain during 1960, and a Japanese affiliate began manufacture in 1963.

have been split into two groups each, so as to furnish a wider range of experience.

Diagram 6–8, based on this data, compares the percentage of total world exports supplied by the leading high-wage nations—America, Germany, Britain, and France (and Canada in the synthetic rubbers group)—with the average age of each group.

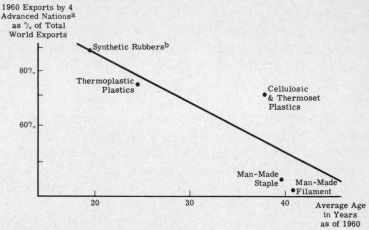

Diagram 6–8. Exports by Advanced Nations vs. Age of Product Group
(*a*) America, Germany, Britain, France. (*b*) Also Canada.

This diagram offers further evidence that the advanced nations specialise in the newer groups of synthetics.

Diagram 6–9, also based on this data, plots the percentage of world production which entered trade in 1960 against average group age. Clearly a larger fraction of younger synthetic materials entered world commerce. Exports of older goods meet considerable local resistance, since many nations have already begun manufacture. On the other hand, young products usually confront virgin markets. Thus not only do the most advanced countries specialize in the newest of products, but also the bulk of world trade is concentrated in such goods.

This conclusion, in conjunction with our earlier analysis of pricing behaviour (Chapter 1), points to a reconsideration of gains-from-trade theory. For insofar as gains-from-trade theory concerns itself with factor incomes and the ability easily to win export markets, Posner's trade theory may imply a most uneven distribution of benefits. Unfortunately, resources and space did not permit investigation of this interesting possibility.

Statistical Analysis. Appendix C presents the full statistical analysis. Briefly, the analysis attempts to explain national export shares (of world exports) by four independent variables: the

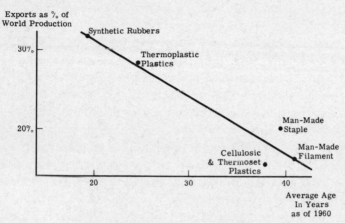

Diagram 6–9. Exports vs. Age of Product Group

imitation lag, wage levels, the size of home markets (as measured by gross domestic product), and the accumulated volume of past production. Synthetic materials were divided into two groups for the analysis: plastics and synthetic rubbers on the one hand, and man-made fibres on the other. Synthetic rubbers were not analysed separately from plastics because of the small number of nations yet exporting synthetic rubbers. For the plastics and synthetic rubbers group, sixteen countries were analysed; for the man-made fibres group, twenty-one countries. Each group was analysed for the years 1952, 1957, and 1962. Earlier years were not examined because of the paucity of data. Imports were ignored because of the distorting effect of different national tariff levels.

The imitation lag proved consistently useful in explaining export shares. Home market size helped explain shares of plastics and synthetic rubbers trade, but not man-made fibres, while the converse was true of the wage level. Accumulated past production proved somewhat useful for both product groups. However, we tentatively concluded that accumulated past production does not explain *dynamic* scale economies so much as *static* scale economies. This suggestion, it should be noted, conflicts with Posner's hypothesis set forth in Chapter 1. Perhaps the length of time in production (Kaldor's hypothesis) better accounts for the development of technology than mere volume of production. Since the wage variable was useful in explaining man-made fibres trade in only one year—1962—we may conclude that, as yet, low-wage trade has not been very important. As the man-made fibres group grows older, such trade may occupy a greater role.

Typically, the regression equations explained about 90% of the variance in national export shares. The partial correlation coefficients between the imitation lag and exports ranged from -0.455 to -0.820. Home market size, as measured by gross domestic product, exhibited partial correlation coefficients ranging from 0.345 to 0.911 with respect to plastics and synthetic rubbers exports. Past production partial correlation coefficients ranged from 0.216 to 0.525. (See Table C–13.) In relating past production to past lags and past income, it became clear that past income has exercised greater influence. Thus, most of the effect of past production upon export shares should be attributed to the benefit of having enjoyed a large home market in past years.

We had hoped that the statistical analysis of export shares would permit an approximate division between technological gap trade on the one hand and scale economy trade on the other. However, home market sizes and imitation lags are highly correlated: the simple correlation coefficients between these two variables always exceeded 75%. The multiple regression equations could not, therefore, be safely used to separate trade between the two theories. In an ill-fated attempt to overcome the high correlation between the two most important independent variables, *changes* in export shares were compared with *changes* in imitation lags, home market sizes, wages, and past production volumes for the periods 1952–57 and 1957–62. This analysis of export share changes was predicated on two assumptions: first, that the independent variables would be less highly correlated with each other; and second, that a statistical explanation of export share changes would also explain absolute export shares. As it turned out, only the income and past production parameters were statistically significant, in contrast to the results from analysing absolute export shares. Accordingly, the question of inter-correlation between the independent variables did not arise. The only conclusion which could be safely drawn from the analysis of export changes is that changes in home market size and past production —both of which enable greater static scale economy exploitation —have primarily determined recent export share changes. To put this conclusion in another light, the developing nations which recently commenced production of some synthetic materials, thus reducing their imitation lags, have not correspondingly expanded their exports. For at the same time the developed nations (whose market sizes have grown more rapidly) have more thoroughly exploited static scale economies.

Our analysis therefore failed in its attempt quantitatively to distinguish technological gap trade from scale economy trade. Both are important, and in recent years, as product groups have aged, scale economy trade may be gaining greater prominence. But aside from the clues which may be gleaned from the partial correlation coefficients, we cannot be more precise.

REFERENCES

1. Japanese official export statistics; *Rubber Statistical Bulletin*, April 1961.

2. A. Egendorf, Jr., "The Pure Theory of International Trade", suggests that the multiple regression analysis may understate low-wage trade for aggregation reasons.

3. D. C. Hague, *The Economics of Man-Made Fibres*, 1957, p. 57. Also cf. C. P. Kindleberger, *Foreign Trade and the National Economy*, 1962, Chapter 6.

4. The United Kingdom trade statistics hide polyethylene exports in a basket category because of the dominant position of I.C.I.

5. *Modern Plastics*, January 1964.

6. *Ibid.*

7. In other words, factor-intensity (an important focus in the factor proportions account) might very well supplement the themes of the technological gap theory. This possibility is investigated at greater length in my thesis, *Synthetic Materials: A Study in International Trade* 1963 (Cambridge University Library).

Chapter 7

CONCLUSIONS

SYNTHETIC materials production belongs to a new class of science-oriented "footloose" industries. In light of this independence from natural resource location, our study has examined three rival trade explanations: the factor proportions account, the scale economy account, and the technological gap account. Our major finding was that the scale economy theory and the technological gap theory together explain most synthetic materials commerce. The factor proportions theory did not prove relevant to this branch of trade.

The factor proportions account essentially views trade flows as a function of international factor price ratio differences. International wage differences, however, so exceed international profit differences that, under the assumptions of the factor proportions theory, low-wage countries enjoy a comparative advantage in manufacturing almost any synthetic material. But the actual flow of trade directly contradicts this finding: high-wage countries are responsible for most synthetic materials exports.

The scale economy account was perhaps the simplest theory considered by our study. This account rests on two basic conditions: increasing returns to scale (using a given technique), and sufficient trade barriers so that home market size roughly determines national exploitation of scale economies. Increasing returns to scale characterise nearly all synthetic materials, although they are greater among plastics and synthetic rubbers than among man-made fibres. And artificial barriers—tariffs and quotas—do ensure that the size of home markets influences the exploitation of static scale economies. Statistical investigation revealed that the size of home markets, as measured by gross domestic product, exercises a rather greater influence on plastics and synthetic rubbers trade than on man-made fibres trade. This result bears out the incidence of scale economies found in the various branches of the industry.

The technological gap account occupied the central position in our study. This theory relates both the exploitation of static scale economies and the improvement of technology to the date when a nation first undertakes production. The technological gap account asserts that the country which first begins production will usually enjoy the best technology and harvest the greatest static scale economies. Initially this country should have large exports and practically no imports. The innovating country's trade position will, however, change with the passage of time. Quite likely the innovating country will be an advanced high-wage nation. As production of the new good spreads to other nations, many of which pay lower industrial wages, her "technological gap" exports should decline. And when low-wage imitating nations finally acquire proper technology and build sufficiently large plants, they may reverse the flow of trade and send "low-wage" exports to the innovating country. The technological gap theory thus encompasses a sequential dichotomy between technological gap trade and low-wage trade.

Technological gap trade rests not on lower unit factor costs, but on better factor utilisation resulting from technological superiority and greater exploitation of static scale economies. There was some question whether technological superiority results primarily from a large volume of past production, or from a long history of production experience. The available evidence favoured the latter explanation (Kaldor's hypothesis). Not only are plant costs closely related to imitation lags, but also the statistical evidence suggests that past production may be primarily linked to the exploitation of *static* scale economies. However, the question was by no means resolved by the available data.

The age-composition of exports from advanced countries indirectly confirmed the presence of technological gap trade. Exports from a collection of advanced countries were found to be heavily biased in favour of new products by comparison with the exports from other countries. Total synthetic materials exports were likewise biased by comparison with total world production, suggesting the importance of technological gap commerce.

In contrast to technological gap trade, low-wage trade rests on a unit factor cost advantage: that is, on the lower wages of less advanced nations. When the advantage of lower wages overcomes the disadvantages of technological and scale economy inferiority, low-wage trade supersedes technological gap trade. It was found, however, that low-wage trade has not occupied a major position in synthetic materials commerce. According to the multiple regression approach, only man-made fibres commerce proved responsive to the level of wage rates, and only in the year 1962 was the wage parameter statistically significant. According to the trade classification approach, small amounts of low-wage trade have characterised all synthetic materials, and the amounts were smaller when the product group was younger.

The technological gap theory and the scale economy theory thus both proved relevant to synthetic materials experience. But it is not possible to say which theory accounted for a larger fraction of trade. The technological gap theory does not, however, depend upon artificial trade barriers. One may therefore speculate that a free trade world would witness an expanded role for technological gap trade as opposed to scale economy trade.

Much work remains to be done on the technological gap theory.* More sophisticated statistical analysis, embodying a wide range of industries and different trade variables, is especially demanded. It should be particularly interesting to investigate the effects of average product age and average factor intensity on trade flows. Certainly the characteristics and mechanisms of industry spread require further study.

We have throughout avoided discussing the gains-from-trade, or the subsidiary question of tariff policy. But the technological gap account intimately affects this aspect of international economic theory. Perhaps the most important questions lie in that area of economic thought.

* As this book was going to press, the author learned of papers by G. K. Douglass, Pomona College, and A. Egendorf, Jr., Harvard College, and of a dissertation by S. Hirsch, Harvard Business School. Douglass, in "Innovation and International Trade", has examined the application of the theory to the motion-picture industry, with positive results. He plans a further study of the transistor industry. Egendorf, in "The Pure Theory of International Trade" and "Analysis", has critically examined the statistical technique and conceptual approaches developed in this book, and has suggested some fresh approaches. Hirsch, in *Location of Industry and International Competitiveness*, has re-examined the theoretical structure and applied it to branches of the electronics industry; an excerpt from his thesis is published in the November 1965 *National Institute Economic Review*.

Appendix A

TRANSPORT COSTS

TRANSPORT economies are usually a minor force in determining the national location of synthetic materials production. Synthetic materials production may thus be fairly categorised as a "footloose" industry. This proposition is easily demonstrated. Table A–1 shows shipping distances between representative ports. The left-hand column lists ports which might supply basic raw materials:

Table A–1. Shipping Distances between Representative Ports

Port of Origin	Bombay	Buenos Aires	Cape Town	Lagos	Le Havre	New York	Sydney	Yokohama
Abadan	3		11		12		14	13
Jakarta	5						7	6
LeHavre	11[a]	11	11	7		6	21	20
Maracaibo		9	11	9	8	4		
New Orleans		12	14	9	9	3	17	
New York	15[a]	11	13	10	6		18	18[b]
Vancouver	18						13	8
Yokohama	10		16				8	

(Port of Destination spans the eight destination columns.)

Source: *The Mercantile Marine Atlas,* 1959.
Only relevant distances cited. 1000 kilometres = 540 nautical miles.
(a) Suez Canal Route.   (b) Panama Canal Route.

New York, Le Havre, and Yokohama for coal; Abadan, Maracaibo, New Orleans, and Jakarta for petroleum; New Orleans and Yokohama for sulphur; Vancouver and New York for wood pulp. Across the top, Table A–1 lists port areas which are actual or potential synthetic materials manufacturing regions. In most cases, as this table illustrates, manufacturing regions may obtain the basic resources for producing synthetics by voyages in the neighbourhood of ten thousand kilometres. During the 1950s, basic chemical resources incurred freight rates of rather less than $4 per thousand kilometre-metric ton, including handling charges.[1]

As a model to evaluate the transport cost burden, let us assume that Country A, which is ten thousand kilometres by sea from Country B, has all the basic resources and Country B has none, and that in producing a typical synthetic material, half the weight of basic resources is lost during processing.[2] Each metric ton of synthetic material manufactured in Country B from resources exported by Country A thus incurs $40 extra cost for the shipment of wasted basic resources ($4 per thousand kilometre-metric ton times ten thousand kilometres). In recent years plastics and synthetic rubbers have been priced at about $700 per metric ton and man-made fibres at about $1,500 per metric ton.[3] Hence Country B's transport disadvantage of $40 per metric ton amounts to only 6% on plastics and synthetic rubbers, and 3% on man-made fibres. Considering that the underlying weight loss and freight rate estimates err on the side of exaggeration, and that far greater cost differences may arise for other reasons, these disadvantages are insignificant.[4]

REFERENCES

1. W. Isard, *et al.*, *Industrial Complex Analysis*, 1959, pp. 109–116; private communication, Chamber of Shipping of the United Kingdom, July 1963. The Chamber's index of tramp freight rates suggests that rates were much lower prior to the Second World War, and somewhat lower in the 1960s.

2. Few synthetic materials require as much as double their weight in scarce basic resources. See Chapter 3 and Appendix B in my thesis, *Synthetic Materials: A Study in International Trade*, 1963 (Cambridge University Library).

3. U.S. Tariff Commission, *Synthetic Organic Chemicals*, various issues; Textile Economics Bureau, *Textile Organon*, various issues. Higher prices prevailed prior to the Second World War.

4. My thesis, *op. cit.*, examines the transport cost burden in greater detail, but arrives at the same conclusion.

FACTOR-INTENSITY REVERSALS

BAGICHA S. MINHAS has contended that "the phenomenon of goods that interchange their roles of being capital intensive seems to be general enough to be empirically important".[1] In other words, Minhas casts doubt on the empirical validity of the "strong factor-intensity hypothesis". According to this hypothesis, industry factor-intensity ranking is not much influenced by factor price ratios. Thus, the lists of twenty industries ranked by capital-intensity in countries with widely different wage : profit ratios, such as the United States and Japan, should be tolerably similar. If not, then important factor-intensity "reversals" occur between the two countries: some goods which are capital-intensive in America are labour-intensive in Japan, and vice-versa.

Minhas' case for the empirical importance of factor-intensity reversals rests, first on a deductive examination of CES (constant elasticity of substitution) or "homohypallagic" production functions, and second on a comparison of United States and Japanese capital-intensities. A general form of the homohypallagic production function is:[2]

$$V_i - v_i \left[\delta_i K^{-\beta_i} + (\mathbf{1} + \delta_i) l^{-\beta_i} \right]^{-1/\beta_i}$$

where V_i is value added by industry i; K and L stand for capital and labour; and v_i, δ_i, and β_i are the parameters. For this class of production functions the elasticity of substitution between capital and labour in industry i, σ_i, is given by the expression:[3]

$$\sigma_i = \frac{\mathbf{1}}{\beta_i + \mathbf{1}}$$

It is undeniable that if homohypallagic production functions characterise technology, and if different industries exhibit different elasticities of substitution between capital and labour, "the reversal of relative factor-intensity is as inevitable as the meeting of two straight lines with different slopes"[4]—*provided* that factor price ratios differ sufficiently between the two countries. For the sake of argument, let us accept that homohypallagic production functions accurately describe technological alternatives, and that elasticities of substitution do differ between industries. Nonetheless, those factor-intensity reversals which characterise industrial experience need not necessarily have major empirical significance. For it requires a large factor price ratio difference to induce an important reversal unless elasticities of substitution differ substantially between industries. Diagram B–1 illustrates the relationship between substitution differences and reversals.

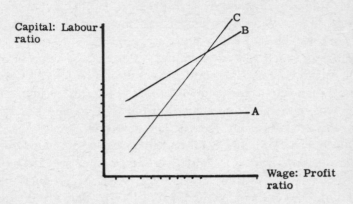

Diagram B–1.   Factor Intensity Reversals

Capital : labour ratios and wage : profit ratios are both plotted on logarithmic scales; hence the slopes indicate substitution elasticities. Since elasticities differ substantially between industries A and C, a small wage : profit ratio difference can induce a major factor-intensity reversal. That is to say, within a small wage : profit ratio range, industry A can change from being significantly more capital-intensive than industry C to being significantly less capital-intensive. But since substitution elasticities are similar between industries B and C, a reversal of the same quantitative magnitude requires a much larger wage : profit ratio difference. Minhas himself observes that, for the majority of industries, elasticities only "range from approximately 0·70 to a little over 1".[5] Thus, there is some question whether reversals will be important within the observable wage : profit ratio range.

To resolve this question, Minhas compares United States and Japanese capital-intensities in twenty industries, using 1947

United States data, and 1951 Japanese data. The American wage : profit ratio in the early 1950s was about $3,600 : 15%, or, to express it in a single figure, $24,000, while the Japanese ratio was $400 : 22%, or $1,800. International differences in wage : profit ratios primarily arise from wage differences, since industrial profit rates are much the same from one country to another. As Minhas points out, profit rates "range from 22 to 15 per cent per annum" while wage rates extend from $250 per annum in the impoverished Asian countries to $3,600 per annum in North America.[6] Because profit rates do not vary greatly, the wage : profit ratios $24,000 (U.S.) and $1,800 (Japan) represent, for all practical purposes, the extreme wage : profit ratios embodied in manufactured goods trade in the early 1950s. For at that time, very few exports of manufactures originated in countries with industrial wages lower than Japan, while no exports originated in countries with wages higher than the United States.[7] Since the wage : profit ratio difference between these two countries was very nearly the maximum possible, the scope for major factor-intensity reversals was also very nearly the maximum. Between other pairs of nations we should thus expect factor-intensity reversals to be less important than between Japan and America, inasmuch as wage : profit ratio differences would normally be smaller. Hence, unless major reversals are revealed in Minhas' data, it can be justifiably concluded (pending further evidence) that the strong factor-intensity hypothesis furnished a not unreasonable description of the international economy during the early 1950s.

Measuring capital-intensity according to total factor inputs (direct plus indirect), Minhas finds a Spearman rank correlation of 0·328 between Japan and America; measuring it according to direct inputs only, he finds a correlation of 0·730.[8] Minhas, however, includes agriculture in his list of twenty "industries". And agriculture is the *third* most capital-intensive "industry" in America, but *twentieth* in Japan, on the basis of total factor requirements; likewise it is *third* in America, but *fourteenth* in Japan on the basis of direct factor requirements. This disparity between the rank position of agriculture in the two countries largely accounts for the low correlations which Minhas finds.

The inclusion of agriculture in an industry factor-intensity ranking is surely inappropriate. While the strong factor-intensity hypothesis purports to describe production conditions for industry considered alone, or for agriculture considered alone, it does not pretend to describe the behaviour of factor relations in a mixed bag of industry and agriculture. Agriculture embodies large amounts of land, and thus should not be included in a ranking which centres on the two factors of production, capital and labour.

Table B–1. Industry Ranking by Capital-Intensity

Industry	Ranks Based on Total Capital & Labour Inputs		Ranks Based on Direct Capital & Labour Inputs	
	U.S.A.	Japan	U.S.A.	Japan
Petroleum Products	1	1	1	1
Coal Products	2	2	2	2
Non-ferrous Metals	4	4	3	3
Iron & Steel	5	3	4	5
Chemicals	3	5	5	4
Paper & Products	6	11	6	14
Non-metallic Mineral Products	7	9	7	11
Grain Mill Products	—	—	8	6
Processed Foods	—	—	9	7
Transport Equipment	9	10	10	9
Machinery	10	6	11	10
Shipbuilding	12	7	12	8
Rubber & Products	11	12	13	15
Lumber & Wood	13	16	14	16
Printing & Publishing	15	8	15	17
Industry (not elsewhere classified)	14	15	16	19
Textiles	8	14	17	12
Leather	16	17	18	18
Apparel	17	13	19	13

Source: B. S. Minhas, *op. cit.*, p. 147, with emendations as described herein.

Low land : labour ratios, as in Japan, may well preclude high capital : labour ratios, particularly when land tenure is characterised by small holdings unsuited for mechanised methods. Moreover, the composition of agricultural output differs enormously between Japan and America. Japan concentrates on labour-intensive rice and sericulture; America concentrates on capital-intensive wheat, corn, and cotton.[9] These various considerations suggest that agriculture should be removed from Minhas' industry list.

After removing agriculture, the industry ranking appears as in Table B–1. Grain mill products and processed foods have been omitted from the total factor requirements ranking because, when viewed as vertically integrated enterprises, these two industries are quite heavily influenced by agricultural factor-intensity. The Spearman rank correlation between the two countries is then 0·765 when capital-intensity is measured according to total factor inputs, and 0·833 when measured according to direct factor inputs. Considering the large difference between United States and Japanese factor price ratios, the strong factor-intensity hypothesis seems to describe the international economy of the early 1950s more accurately than the alternative supposition of widespread reversals. Indeed, were reversals truly the dominant characteristic, negative correlations would be found. As it happens, the correlations are strongly positive.

Similarly, an examination of L. Rostas' data comparing horse-power per worker for 24 industries in the United States (1929) and the United Kingdom (1930) offers much support for the strong factor intensity hypothesis.[10] Even though horsepower per worker is not entirely adequate as a measure of capital per worker, the industry Spearman rank correlation between the two countries was no less than 0·957.

REFERENCES

1. B. S. Minhas, "The Homohypallagic Production Function," *Journal of Political Economy*, April 1962, p. 147.
2. *Op. cit.*, p. 154.
3. *Op. cit.*, p. 142.
4. *Op. cit.*, p. 143.
5. *Op. cit.*, p. 143, footnote 18
6. *Op. cit.*, p. 146.
7. Even as late as 1955, exports of manufactures from countries with lower industrial wages than Japan only amounted to about 10% of total exports of manufactures (Soviet bloc excluded). A. Maizels, *Industrial Growth and World Trade*, Appendix A, 1963; United Nations, *Commodity Trade Statistics*, 1955.
8. Minhas, *op. cit.*, pp. 146–8.
9. In 1951, about 50% (by value) of United States agricultural output consisted of wheat, corn, and cotton; in the same year, over 80%

(by value) of Japanese agricultural output consisted of rice and silk. Food and Agriculture Organisation, *Yearbook of Agricultural Statistics*, 1952; United Nations, *National Income and Its Distribution in Under-Developed Countries*, 1951; U.S. Dept. of Commerce, *Statistical Abstract of the United States*, 1952.

10. L. Rostas, *Comparative Productivity in British and American Industry*, 1948.

Appendix C

STATISTICAL ANALYSIS

OUR statistical analysis attempts to explain national export shares; that is, national exports related to total world exports. The export share* was selected for explanation because our interest lies in discovering what strengthens a nation's performance *vis-à-vis* other nations.†

Plastic and synthetic rubber exports are examined as one large group, while man-made fibre exports are treated separately. Synthetic rubbers are combined with plastics because so far there are not sufficient synthetic rubber exporting nations to justify analysing that group alone.

The statistical analysis is confined to the years 1952, 1957, and 1962. Sixteen nations were analysed for plastics and synthetic rubbers, while 21 nations were analysed for man-made fibres. Figures pertinent to the analysis are given in Tables C–1 through C–9. Owing both to unreliable data and the disruption caused by World War II, years prior to 1952 could not be usefully analysed.

It may be asked why imports are not also examined. Unfortunately, varying levels of tariff protection in different parts of the world work to obscure whatever indication imports might give as to the nature of comparative advantage.‡ Brazilian plastics imports are meagre, while German plastics imports are substantial, but that reflects tariff barriers, not comparative advantage.

---

* More precisely, the variable used was national exports divided by average exports for trading nations. This variable, of course, differs from the national export share only by a constant multiple.

† The export share variable may, however, exaggerate scale economy trade. Egendorf contends that Country A, which is twice as big as Country B, should approximately account for twice as big a share of world export markets, quite apart from any scale economy advantages. If analysis focused on a trade variable which accepted this contention (such as the synthetic materials share of each country's manufactures exports), then the role of home market size would certainly appear smaller than in our presentation. In any event, there is considerable doubt in my own mind whether the export share variable truly reflects *comparative* advantage, even though it seems like the appropriate variable in the technological gap context.

‡ According to the reasoning of the scale economy theory, tariffs affect exports as well as imports. But exports are influenced through the workings of comparative advantage, while imports are influenced without regard to comparative advantage. The tentative analysis in my thesis suggests, however, that more detailed examination of imports would substantiate the features brought out by our export analysis.

Four different regression equation forms (with the same explanatory variables in each) were tried:

(1a) *Linear* $\quad X_t = K + aL_t + bW_t + cY_t + d\sum\limits_{0}^{t-1} f(\lambda)P$

(1b) *Semi-Log* $\quad \text{Log}X_t = K + aL_t + bW_t + cY_t + d\sum\limits_{0}^{t-1} f(\lambda)P$

(1c) *Double Log* $\quad \text{Log}X_t = K + a\text{Log}L_t + b\text{Log}W_t$
$$+ c\text{Log}Y_t + d\text{Log}\sum\limits_{0}^{t-1} f(\lambda)P$$

(1d) *Semi-Log,* $\quad \text{Log}X_t = K + aL_t + bW_t + c\text{Log}Y_t$
Double Log
Combination $\qquad\qquad + d\text{Log}\sum\limits_{0}^{t-1} f(\lambda)P$

Where:

t denotes the year under examination;

X is the national volume of exports in metric tons divided by the average of exports for all exporting nations (Tables C–1 and C–2);

L is the national imitation lag in years divided by the average of the imitation lags of all exporting nations (Table C–3);

W is the national level of chemical wages in United States dollars divided by the average level of chemical wages in exporting nations (Table C–4);

Y is the national gross domestic product in billions of United States dollars at 1955 prices divided by the average gross domestic product of exporting nations (Table C–5);

P is national production of the synthetic material divided by the average production of exporting nations (Tables C–8, C–9);

$f(\lambda)$ is a weighting function which assigns decreasing importance to production which occurred a longer time ago;

$a, b, c,$ and d are parameters; if the equation is meaningful, a and b must be less than zero, while c and d must be greater than zero;

K is a constant.

Form (1a), the simple linear form, yielded the highest multiple correlation coefficients. This is evident from Table C–10 which presents the multiple correlation coefficients (R^2) obtained for each form using various values of lambda (0·50, 0·75, 0·90, 0·95, 1·00). The linear form usually gave higher correlation coefficients, regardless of the value of lambda, than the other forms. Comparing correlation coefficients on a year-by-lambda-value basis, the linear form proved superior in fifteen cases, the semi-log, double-log form proved superior in ten cases, and the double-log form proved superior in the remaining five cases. If the multiple correlation coefficients are averaged by equation form and lambda value (bottom of Table C–10), the linear form shows itself best for each lambda value.

When lambda was set equal to 1·00, the linear form yielded the best average results, though only marginally better than when lambda was set equal to 0·95. It should be noted that the lambda value 0·95 proved superior to 1·00 in three instances out of six, and overall was insignificantly less good than 1·00. However, since we want to deal with the equation form which yields the best overall multiple correlation coefficient, our statistical evaluation rests on the linear form with lambda equal 1·00. Now let us consider what this equation says.

First, each nation's performance with respect to the explanatory variables is measured against the average performance of competing nations. In the battle for export markets, the nation's absolute level of wages is not so important as its level of wages relative to competing countries; and likewise with the other elements of comparative advantage.

Second, the equation suggests that a longer imitation lag and a higher wage level both *decrease* the nation's export share. These two variables (L and W) clearly pertain to the technological gap theory.

Third, the equation asserts that a larger home market (Y, measured by gross domestic product) and a larger accumulated backlog of production ($\sum_{0}^{t-1} f(\lambda)P$) both *enhance* the nation's export share. It follows directly from the postulates of the scale economy theory that a larger home market would assist exports by abetting the harvest of static scale economies. Moreover, Chapters 1 and 2 pointed to accumulated past production as one hypothesis which might explain dynamic scale economies. But we did not automatically suppose that a given percentage of world production undertaken in 1930 exercises the same influence on 1962 exports as that same percentage of production would exercise if undertaken in 1960. Indeed, the weighting function attached to past production, $f(\lambda)$, was intended to diminish the importance of "older" past production. The weighting function was arbitrarily assigned the form:

$$f(\lambda)P = \lambda P_{-1} + \lambda^2 P_{t-2} + \lambda^3 P_{t-3} + \dots + \lambda^n P_{t-n}; \ 0 \leq \lambda \leq 1$$

As noted earlier, the values of lambda tried were 0·50, 0·75, 0·90, 0·95, and 1·00. The last value, 1·00, in fact proved to be marginally better than the alternatives.

In other words, a given percentage of world production undertaken in 1930 appears to exercise very nearly equal influence on 1962 exports as that same percentage of production exercises if undertaken in 1960.

Table C–11 presents the parameters obtained, by year and product group, using the linear form. Evidently the parameters often exhibit the wrong sign. For example, the wage parameter for plastics and synthetic rubbers in 1962 is 0·0198, whereas theory predicts that this parameter should be negative. Whenever parameters did exhibit the wrong sign, they were dropped and the remaining parameters recomputed. Sometimes the initial recomputation called for further parameter elimination as other wrong-signed parameters cropped up. Table C–12 presents the results of these revisions, together with parameter confidence ranges (in parentheses). The confidence ranges are computed for the 70% level; that is, they show the range within which we can be 70% certain that the parameter falls. Ordinarily, parameter confidence ranges are quoted for the 95% certainty level. Our departure from standard practice is justified by the erratic nature of foreign commerce, and the primitive level of empirical analysis yet prevailing in this field.*

* Confidence ranges were calculated using Student's t test. F. A. Graybill, *An Introduction to Linear Statistical Models*, Volume I, 1961, p. 127, suggests that the F test is more appropriate when two or more explanatory variables appear in the same regression equation.

From Table C–12 it can be seen that the wage parameters for man-made fibres for 1952 and 1957 are not significantly different from zero at the 70% level. Accordingly, in Table C–13 these two parameters are dropped, and the remaining parameters, together with their confidence levels, are recomputed. Those parameters not significantly different from zero at the 95% level (the standard test) are asterisked. It will be noticed that only two parameters fall in that category. Table C–13 also presents partial correlation coefficients and multiple correlation coefficients (R).

Some interesting features emerge from Table C–13. Foremost, one sees that only the lag parameter proved consistently significant—a remarkable tribute to the technological gap theory. The size of home markets held some explanatory value for plastics and synthetic rubber exports, but none for man-made fibres. This dichotomy is reasonable, since static scale economies do not loom so large in man-made fibres manufacturing. Conversely, wage levels contributed somewhat to the explanation of man-made fibres trade, but nothing to plastics and synthetic rubbers trade. Again this could be expected, since man-made fibres are an older product group in which wage levels should—under the technological gap theory—exercise greater influence. Especially was this true in 1962 when the average age of man-made fibres stood at 40·2 years, a record level. Interestingly, as the wage parameter grows larger and more significant in explaining fibres exports (cf. Table C–12), the lag parameter assumes a smaller role. This inverse movement confirms the technological gap theory: with the passage of time, wages become more important, while dynamic scale economies and a head-start become less so.

Past production helped explain trade in both product groups. But it is not immediately apparent why past production was a more useful variable in later years. One line of speculation suggests itself, however. Possibly large past production is more closely related to the exploitation of *static* scale economies than *dynamic* scale economies. And perhaps dynamic scale economies are best accounted for by the length of time in production (the imitation lag) rather than the volume of past production. If so, this would explain the improved significance, in later years, of the past production parameter. For with the passing of years technology becomes more similar between nations. Accordingly, static scale economies (and wage rates) assume increasing importance in determining the locus of comparative advantage. If, then, past production primarily indicates exploitation of static scale economies, the observed results are only logical.

The foregoing speculation suggests that past production supplements the size of home markets in explaining the harvest of static scale economies. Insofar as large past production depends upon a history of short imitation lags, then a large partial correlation coefficient for the d parameter in equation $(1a)$ sustains the technological gap theory. But if a history of large national income primarily explains past production volume, then the mechanisms of the scale economy account are most important. To sort out these two influences, the volume of past production was related to the magnitude of past lags and the magnitude of past income:

$$(2) \quad \sum_{0}^{t-1} P = e \sum_{0}^{t-1} L + f \sum_{0}^{t-1} Y$$

Equation (2) is linear, and the explanatory variables are unweighted sums. Perhaps some weighting function, such as was used in assessing the influence of past production on exports, would yield better results. But resources did not warrant an investigation into this possibility. Table C–14 presents the partial correlation coefficients from analysing past production of both product groups for the year 1962. Past income exercised greater influence upon the magnitude of past production than did past lags. In other words, the size of home markets primarily determines the size of output. The influence of past lags was not, however, negligible. Past income and past lags together explained more than 95% of the variance in past production.

One goal of our statistical analysis was to suggest an approximate division between the share of synthetic materials commerce accounted for by the technological gap theory and the share accounted for by the scale economy theory. But the strong correlation between the explanatory variables of the two theories renders such a division difficult on the basis of equation $(1a)$.

Table C–15 presents the simple correlation coefficients beween the relevant explanatory variables of equation (1a) (cf. Table C–13). The lag, income, and past production variables, where useful in explaining trade, consistently showed a better than 70% correlation between themselves. Only the wage variable was not highly correlated with the others, but wages were not very useful in explaining trade. Since a division of trade between the various theories on the basis of equation (1a) was precluded by the high correlations between the independent variables, the problem was attacked from another angle.

The following difference equation was derived from equation (1a):

$$(3) \quad \Delta X = K + \dot{a}\Delta L + \dot{b}\Delta W + \dot{c}\Delta Y + \dot{d}\Delta \sum_0^{t-1} f(\lambda)P$$

The variables and the parameters are the same as before, except that the dot notation (e.g. $\dot{c}$) indicates that the parameters pertain to year-to-year changes. It was hoped that an examination of changes in export shares over five-year periods—1952–57 and 1957–62—via equation (3) would enable an approximate division of trade between the technological gap theory and the scale economy theory. This hope was predicated on two assumptions: first, that correlations between *changes* in the independent variables would be significantly smaller than correlations between the absolute levels of the independent variables; and second, that an equation which explains marginal changes in exports would also adequately explain the absolute value of exports. Table C–16 presents the parameters derived from equation (3). Frequently the parameters exhibited the wrong sign. For example, three times out of four, changes in the imitation lag were positively correlated with export changes. In Table C–17, the variables with wrong-signed parameters were dropped, and the remaining, recomputed, parameters are presented with 70% confidence levels. Finally, in Table C–18, only those parameters significantly different from zero at the 70% confidence level are presented, together with 70% confidence limits, and partial correlation coefficients.

On the basis of Table C–18, only income and past production are helpful in explaining changes in export shares. The table thus does not provide much assistance in separating technological gap trade from scale economy trade—unless we reject the former theory and assume that all trade is scale economy trade. This assumption, however, seems unwarranted. For while changes in export shares may be unrelated to changes in lags, it does not follow that absolute export shares are unrelated to absolute lags. Indeed, the results from equation (1a) are quite the contrary. And in parcelling out trade between various theories, it would be misleading to assume that a difference equation explains absolute levels when, in fact, the results from the difference equation conflict with the results from the absolute equation.

An interpretation of Table C–18 which better agrees with the findings of Table C–13 is that imitation lags exercise diminishing importance as product groups advance in age. Consequently, recent changes in national export shares are determined primarily by changes in home market size and past production volume. To put this conclusion another way, the initial technological and marketing advantages of being an early producer yield, in time, to static scale economy advantages. Thus, although many developing nations have lowered their lags relative to the advanced countries, their export shares have failed to grow because North America and Europe have exploited the advantages attending size.

Unfortunately, our statistical analysis has given no concrete separation of trade between the two conflicting theories. We can only conclude that both theories are important, and the static theory becomes more important as product age increases.

Table C-1. Plastics and Synthetic Rubber Exports

Thousand Metric Tons

	1952			1957			1962		
	Plastics	Rubbers	Total	Plastics	Rubbers	Total	Plastics	Rubbers	Total
United States	70·5	33·8	104·3	232·5	203·4	435·9	402·0	303·7	705·7
Germany	23·4	—	23·4	142·6	2·7	145·3	355·0	24·4	389·4
United Kingdom	49·3	—	49·3	124·7	—	124·7	247·0	27·7	274·7
France	5·0	—	5·0	22·3	—	22·3	88·6	23·5	112·1
Italy	3·3	—	3·3	34·0	—	34·0	168·0	40·7	208·7
Japan	1·9	—	1·9	11·0	—	11·0	85·2	6·2	91·4
Canada	7·0	45·0	52·0	22·5	93·4	115·9	34·5	112·5	147·0
Netherlands	4·8	—	4·8	27·6	—	27·6	87·9	39·7	127·6
Sweden	3·7	—	3·7	14·0	—	14·0	45·9	—	45·9
Australia	1·2	—	1·2	1·8	—	1·8	4·3	—	4·3
Belgium	4·1	—	4·1	11·0	—	11·0	42·2	—	42·2
Switzerland	2·7	—	2·7	6·1	—	6·1	21·8	—	21·8
Austria	0·1	—	0·1	1·8	—	1·8	19·8	—	19·8
Spain	—	—	—	—	—	—	1·3	—	1·3
Norway	0·1	—	0·1	2·6	—	2·6	25·2	—	25·2
Denmark	0·4	—	0·4	2·4	—	2·4	11·8	—	11·8

Sources: OECD, *The Chemical Industry in Europe*; *Rubber Statistical Bulletin*; official trade returns.

Table C–2.   Man-Made Fibre Exports

Thousand Metric Tons

	1952	1957	1962
United States	16·3	37·3	73·0
Germany	18·2	88·5	110·1
United Kingdom	18·6	28·1	67·0
France	12·7	22·5	54·2
Italy	22·2	58·0	82·3
Japan	7·3	22·2	78·9
Canada	0·9	2·8	6·9
Netherlands	16·8	26·8	40·3
Sweden	4·1	14·0	19·4
Australia	—	—	0·4
Belgium	12·7	18·6	19·5
Switzerland	12·2	18·6	21·3
Austria	12·7	24·0	37·6
Spain	0·9	0·5	9·6
Norway	10·0	11·3	11·5
Denmark	—	—	0·8
Mexico	—	—	1·0
Finland	4·1	14·0	13·3
Colombia	—	—	2·0
Israel	—	0·1	0·5
Portugal	—	—	0·1

Sources: *Textile Organon*; OECD, *The Textile Industry in Europe*; official trade returns.

Table C-3. First Production Dates

	U.S.A.	Germany	U.K.	France	Italy	Japan	Canada	Nether- lands	Sweden	Australia	Belgium	Switzer- land	Austria	Spain
CELLULOSIC PLASTICS														
1 Cellulose Nitrate (Celluloid)	1870*	1878	1877	1875	1924	1908		1919-35	1932	1949	1935?	1923	1914-31	1940?
2 Cellulose Acetate	1908	1905*	1916	1912	1936	1927		1938?				1940		1960
3 Cellulose Acetate Butyrate	1931*	1935?								1962?	1935?			
4 Ethyl Cellulose	1935	1932*	1940		1939				1944					
5 Methyl Cellulose	1939	1932*				1957								
6 Cellophane	1924	1925	1930	1917*	1946	1929	1932	1957	1935		1925	1934	1951	1949
THERMOSET PLASTICS														
7 Galalith	1919	1899*	1912	1900	1921	1927	1936	1920	1924-39	1934	1937	1931	1925	1935?
8 Phenol Formaldehyde	1909*	1910	1910	1916	1922	1923	1911	1928	1917-54	1928	1934	1937?	1928	1941
9 Urea Formaldehyde	1929	1929	1923*	1930	1936	1935	1945	1940	1941	1938	1938	1937	1947	1947
10 Melamine Formaldehyde	1939	1935*	1938	1955	1951	1951	1949	1955	1945	1946		1937	1955	1960
11 Alkyd	1926*	1927?	1929	1928	1927	1931	1932	1940	1942	1932	1938	1937?	1932	1945
12 Polyester	1942*	1953	1950	1950	1949	1953	1950	1950	1952	1953		1955?	1955	1954
13 Silicone	1941*	1950	1942	1954	1955?	1951						1964*		
14 Epoxy	1947	1955	1945		1958?			1953		1960				
THERMOPLASTIC PLASTICS														
15 Polyvinyl Acetate	1928*	1928*	1949	1937	1954	1936	1931	1955	1955	1949	1949	1942	1958	1957
16 Polyvinyl Chloride	1933	1931*	1940	1940	1951	1939	1942	1949	1945	1950		1942	1953	1950
17 Polyvinyl Alcohol	1938	1928*		1938	1958	1949	1931							1957
18 Polyvinyl Butyral	1937*	1948		1942	1960	1944								1962
19 Polyvinylidene Chloride (Saran)	1940*		1950	1951	1942	1950								
20 Polystyrene	1933	1930*	1954	1951	1954	1957	1946		1950	1953				1958
21 Polystyrene/Styrene/Butadiene	1947	1942*		1954			1954		1952	1953				1958
22 Polystyrene/Styrene/Acrylonitrile	1948	1942*	1962?	1962	1962	1963								
23 Acrylonitrile/Butadiene/Styrene	1946*	1955	1962	1960	1952	1954	1954							
24 High Pressure Polyethylene	1941	1944	1937*	1954	1954*	1958	1957	1959	1963	1957	1962?			1963?
25 Linear Polyethylene	1956	1955	1959	1955				1962						
26 Polypropylene	1957*	1957*	1959	1960	1957*	1961	1964?	1962	1963				1960	
27 Polymethyl Methacrylate	1936	1930*	1933	1938	1937	1938		1961	1950				1959	1950?
28 Nylon	1941*	1943	1950	1943	1946?	1953	1957	1950				1944		
29 Fluoroethylene	1943*	1958	1945	1958	1955	1963					1955?	1953		
30 Acetal	1953*					1963		1961						
31 Polycarbonate	1957*	1957*				1955								

(continued)

Table C–3. *(continued)*

	U.S.A.	Germany	U.K.	France	Italy	Japan	Canada	Nether-lands	Sweden	Australia	Belgium	Switzer-land	Austria	Spain
SYNTHETIC RUBBERS														
32 Methyl Butadiene	1930*	1915-19												
33 Polysulfide	1931*	b	1941-45											
34 Neoprene	1941*	1956	1960	1956		1934-45	1943-44	1960		1961				
35 Styrene	1939	1955b	1958	1960	1957	1962	1943							
36 Nitrile	1942*	1934*	1957	1959	1960	1960	1948							
37 Butyl		b				1959	1944							
38 Polyurethane	1954	1941*	1942	1951	1955	1956	1956	1952	1953		1954			
39 Silicone	1944*	1950	1952	1954?	1961	1953								
40 cis-Polybutadiene	1959*	1963	1964	1954?		1961	1962							1955
41 Hypalon	1951*													
CELLULOSIC MAN-MADE FIBRES														
42 Nitrocellulose Rayon	1921-34	1884-30*	1898-00	1884-30*	1910-25	1908-11					1901-31			1903-13
43 Cuprammonium Rayon	1926	1897*	1904-55	1904-50	1925	1924								1913-16
44 Viscose Rayon:														
44a regular tenacity filament	1905	1901	1900*	1903	1919	1916	1925	1913	1918		1923	1910?	1911?	1916
44b high tenacity filament	1937	1935*	1936	1936	1939	1941	1943	1946	1946	1954	1949	1951	1952	1941
44c staple	1927	1916*	1925	1931	1931	1933	1948	1943	1943		1935	1938	1939	1944
45 Acetate:														
45a filament	1919	1907*	1921	1923	1930	1937	1927			1953	1924			1951
45b staple	1934	1932	1936	1935	1936	1937?	1929*							1951
SYNTHETIC MAN-MADE FIBRES														
46 Nylon:														
46a filament	1938*	1949	1941	1941	1938*	1942	1942	1950		1958	1955	1950		
46b staple	1946	1950	1947	1941*	1942?	1950	1948	1952	1963	1962		1952		
47 Polyvinyl Chloride/Acetate	1936*	1950		1956	1952	1944								
48 Saran	1940*		1949			1953	1954	1952		1960				
49 Polyvinyl Alcohol	1963?					1950*								
50 Protein	1939-58		1937*		1938	1938-42					1939?			
51 Acrylic	1944	1943*	1957	1955	1958	1957	1957	1951	1956		1961			
52 Polyester	1949*	1955	1950	1954	1954	1958	1955	1955						
53 Fluoro-ethylene	1954*		1961											1953
54 Polyethylene	1949*	1956	1951		1957*	1959	1960	1956	1960	1961				1953
55 Polypropylene	1957*		1961		1961	1962	1960			1961				1963
56 Spandex	1958*	c	1962				1963	1963						1961

(continued)

Table C–3. *(continued)*

	Norway	Denmark	Mexico	Finland	Columbia	Israel	Portugal	Brazil**	Argentina**	India**	South Africa**	Chile**	Venezuela**	Turkey**
CELLULOSIC PLASTICS														
2 Cellulose Acetate		1963	1950					1941	1950?	1963		1959		
6 Cellophane			1952	1938	1963			1942	1948	1951				
THERMOSET PLASTICS														
7 Galalith	1935			1921			1935?	1922	1937					
8 Phenol Formaldehyde	1950	1936	1951	1936			1934	1949	1947	1948				
9 Urea Formaldehyde	1950		1947	1943		1953?		1944?	1956?	1951	1961		1960	
10 Melamine Formaldehyde	1951		1962	1955				1958?		1962				
11 Alkyd	1950		1951	1940				1940?						
12 Polyester	1955					1958?		1958	1953	1962	1956	1953?		
14 Epoxy	1954		1957						1958					
THERMOPLASTIC PLASTICS														
15 Polyvinyl Acetate	1956		1952	1950		1961?		1952	1958	1961	1960?			
16 Polyvinyl Chloride	1950		1953			1963		1955	1960	1963	1955			
20 Polystyrene		1960?	1950				1961	1949	1959	1957				
21 Polystyrene/Styrene/Butadiene			1956						1961					
24 High Pressure Polyethylene			1962?			1964?		1958	1962	1959	1964?			
25 Linear Polyethylene		1962	1956					1963						
27 Polymethyl Methacrylate[a]			1956					1949?	1950?					
28 Nylon			1956	1960		1960?		1954						
SYNTHETIC RUBBERS														
35 Styrene			1965?					1960						
CELLULOSIC MAN-MADE FIBRES														
42 Nitrocellulose Rayon	1937		1948	1938	1939		1936	1936–48	1936	1950		1941		1938
44 Viscose Rayon:														
44a regular tenacity filament								1924						
44b high tenacity filament	1946		1953	1954			1963	1948	1948	1961				
44c staple			1952	1938	1951		1954	1938	1944	1954		1959		1938
45 Acetate:														
45a filament			1947					1929	1935	1954			1952	
45b staple			1948					1929*	1935					

(continued)

Table C-3. *(continued)*

	Norway	Denmark	Mexico	Finland	Columbia	Israel	Portugal	Brazil**	Argentina**	India**	South Africa**	Chile**	Venezuela**	Turkey**
SYNTHETIC MAN-MADE FIBRES														
46 Nylon:														
46a filament	1959		1956		1960	1957	1961	1955	1959	1961?		1956	1956	1963
46b staple			1958					1955 1963?						
47 Polyvinyl Chloride/Acetate														
48 Saran			1953			1954								
49 Polyvinyl Alcohol										1963				
51 Acrylic										1964?				
52 Polyester						1963?		1962	1962	1962				
54 Polyethylene	1961?	1962	1959					1962						
55 Polypropylene	1961?		1959			1963?								

Source: G. C. Hufbauer, *Synthetic Materials: A Study in International Trade*, 1963, Appendix A.

(*) Innovating country. (**) Country not included in statistical analysis. (?) Uncertain date.
(a) Plexiglas sheets or molding powder.
(b) Germany manufactured these rubbers before and during the Second World War, but lost her plants to Russia with the cessation of hostilities.
(c) Germany manufactured experimental quantities only during the Second World War. See Chapters 2 and 5.

Table C–4. Approximate Export Weights

Materials	1910	1924	1930	1938/9	1950	1952	1957	1962
Aggregate								
Total Plastics	80?	24	15	26	38	39	49	57
Total Synthetic Rubbers	—	—	—	—	12	20	23	20
Total Man-Made Fibres	20?	76	85	74	50	41	28	23
TOTAL SYNTHETIC MATERIALS	100	100	100	100	100	100	100	100
By Groups								
CELLULOSIC PLASTICS								
1 Cellulose Nitrate (Celluloid)	90	65	38	9	2	$1\frac{1}{2}$	$\frac{1}{2}$	$\frac{1}{4}$
2 Cellulose Acetate	1	2	3	5	4	5	3	2
3 Cellulose Acetate Butyrate	—	—	—	ng	1	1	$\frac{1}{2}$	1
4 Ethyl Cellulose	—	—	—	ng	$\frac{1}{2}$	$\frac{1}{2}$	$\frac{1}{4}$	ng
5 Methyl Cellulose	—	—	—	ng	$\frac{1}{2}$	$\frac{1}{2}$	$\frac{1}{4}$	$\frac{3}{4}$
6 Cellophane	—	ng	8	16	13	8	6	4
THERMOSET PLASTICS								
7 Galalith	6	20	12	5	1	1	$\frac{1}{4}$	ng
8 Phenol Formaldehyde	3	13	29	35	15	9	7	5
9 Urea Formaldehyde	—	—	3	4	8	7	6	5
10 Melamine Formaldehyde	—	—	—	ng	2	3	2	2
11 Alkyd	—	—	6	16	10	7	5	5
12 Polyester	—	—	—	—	1	1	1	2
13 Silicone	—	—	—	—	ng	ng	$\frac{1}{2}$	$\frac{1}{4}$
14 Epoxy	—	—	—	—	ng	$\frac{1}{2}$	$\frac{1}{2}$	1
THERMOPLASTIC PLASTICS								
15 Polyvinyl Acetate	—	—	1	3	2	3	2	3
16 Polyvinyl Chloride	—	—	—	4	17	22	18	21
17 Polyvinyl Alcohol	—	—	—	ng	ng	$\frac{1}{2}$	$\frac{1}{2}$	$\frac{1}{2}$
18 Polyvinyl Butyral	—	—	—	ng	ng	$\frac{1}{2}$	$\frac{1}{4}$	ng
19 Polyvinylidene Chloride (Saran)	—	—	—	—	1	1	1	1
20 Polystyrene	—	—	ng	2	9	11	10	10
21 Polystyrene/Styrene/Butadiene	—	—	—	—	4	4	4	4
22 Polystyrene/Styrene/Acrylonitrile	—	—	—	—	ng	ng	1	$\frac{3}{4}$
23 Acrylonitrile/Butadiene/Styrene	—	—	—	—	ng	ng	$\frac{1}{2}$	$\frac{1}{2}$
24 High Pressure Polyethylene	—	—	—	ng	5	8	20	17
25 Linear Polyethylene	—	—	—	—	—	—	3	6
26 Polypropylene	—	—	—	—	—	—	1	?
27 Polymethyl Methacrylate	—	—	—	1	3	4	4	3
28 Nylon	—	—	—	—	1	1	2	2
29 Fluoroethylene	—	—	—	—	ng	ng	ng	$\frac{1}{2}$
30 Acetal	—	—	—	—	—	ng	ng	$\frac{1}{4}$
31 Polycarbonate	—	—	—	—	—	ng	ng	$\frac{1}{4}$
TOTAL PLASTICS	100	100	100	100	100	100	100	100
SYNTHETIC RUBBERS								
32 Methyl Butadiene	—	—	—	—	—	—	—	—
33 Polysulphide	—	—	ng	ng	ng	ng	—	—
34 Neoprene	—	—	—	ng	7	15	10	12
35 Styrene	—	—	—	ng	80	59	74	70
36 Nitrile	—	—	—	ng	3	11	$6\frac{1}{2}$	4
37 Butyl	—	—	—	—	10	15	9	8
38 Polyurethane	—	—	—	—	ng	ng	$\frac{1}{2}$	3
39 Silicone	—	—	—	—	ng	ng	ng	$\frac{1}{2}$
40 cis-Polybutadiene	—	—	—	—	—	—	—	2
41 Hypalon	—	—	—	—	—	ng	ng	$\frac{1}{2}$
TOTAL SYNTHETIC RUBBERS	—	—	100	100	100	100	100	100

(continued)

Table C–4 *(continued)*

Materials	Approximate Export Weights							
	1910	1924	1930	1938/9	1950	1952	1957	1962
Aggregate								
CELLULOSIC MAN-MADE FIBRES								
42 Nitrocellulose Rayon	30	7	ng	ng	—	—	—	—
43 Cuprammonium Rayon	30	7	3	1	ng	ng	ng	ng
44 Viscose Rayon:								
44a regular tenacity filament	40	84	90	40	28	21	17	12
44b high tenacity filament	—	—	ng	2	11	13	10	7
44c staple	—	ng	2	44	42	47	47	49
45 Acetate:								
45a filament	—	2	5	8	9	8	6	5
45b staple	—	—	ng	5	3	4	3	2
SYNTHETIC MAN-MADE FIBRES								
46 Nylon:								
46a filament	—	—	—	ng	5	4	9	12
46b staple	—	—	—	—	ng	$\frac{1}{2}$	1	1
47 Polyvinyl Chloride/Acetate	—	—	—	ng	1	$\frac{1}{2}$	$\frac{1}{2}$	$\frac{1}{2}$
48 Polyvinylidene Chloride (Saran)	—	—	—	—	ng	$\frac{1}{2}$	1	1
49 Polyvinyl Alcohol	—	—	—	ng	ng	ng	ng	ng
50 Protein	—	—	—	ng	ng	ng	ng	ng
51 Acrylic	—	—	—	—	1	1	3	4
52 Polyester	—	—	—	—	ng	$\frac{1}{2}$	2	4
53 Fluoroethylene	—	—	—	—	—	ng	ng	ng
54 Polyethylene	—	—	—	—	—	—	$\frac{1}{2}$	1
55 Polypropylene	—	—	—	—	—	—	ng	1
56 Spandex	—	—	—	—	—	—	ng	$\frac{1}{2}$
TOTAL MAN-MADE FIBRES	100	100	100	100	100	100	100	100

(—) not produced. (ng) negligible. (?) Rough estimate. The weights refer to tons not value.

Sources: Consult Table C–19.

	1910			1924			1930			1939			1950				
MAXIMUM LAG	Plastics	Man-Made Fibres	Total Synthetics	Plastics	Man-made Fibres	Total Synthetics	Plastics	Man-made Fibres	Total Synthetics	Plastics	Man-made Fibres	Total Synthetics	Plastics	Synthetic Rubbers	Plastics & Rubbers	Man-made Fibres	Total Synthetics
MAXIMUM LAG	36.7	15.7	32.5	42.3	25.2	29.3	34.7	29.4	30.2	27.4	29.3	28.8	26.4	9.8	22.4	35.2	28.8
United States	0.7	1.7	3.3	4.1	9.1	7.9	3.1	6.2	5.7	2.5	8.4	6.8	2.6	0.2	1.7	7.5	4.6
Germany	7.2	6.4	5.8	5.3	0.8	1.9	4.1	0.9	5.7	2.5	0.7	1.2	2.1	9.3	3.9	1.1	2.5
United Kingdom	7.0	5.9	7.6	7.5	3.6	4.5	6.1	1.1	1.9	5.6	5.5	5.5	7.7	max	8.1	5.7	6.9
France	4.6	3.3	4.3	4.5	3.4	3.7	4.5	4.0	4.1	4.6	9.5	8.2	7.4	max	8.0	9.2	8.6
Italy	max	max	max	41.6	20.0	25.2	28.9	19.4	20.8	17.0	16.8	16.4	15.8	max	14.4	14.6	14.5
Japan	34.9	15.1	30.9	31.9	18.5	21.7	23.8	16.6	17.7	14.6	17.0	16.4	12.1	max	11.4	15.6	13.6
Canada	max	max	max	40.7	max	28.5	29.2	24.8	25.5	14.9	22.2	20.3	13.9	3.4	11.5	23.5	17.5
Netherlands	max	max	max	38.3	16.0	21.3	28.8	14.1	16.3	22.5	18.9	19.6	20.4	max	17.9	21.5	19.7
Sweden	max	max	max	41.5	20.2	25.3	30.2	18.6	20.4	18.0	20.9	20.2	16.4	max	14.9	22.9	18.9
Australia	max	max	max	max	max	max	34.1	max	30.1	22.1	max	27.4	20.1	max	17.6	max	26.4
Belgium	max	13.0	32.0	max	22.7	27.8	34.3	22.8	24.5	22.9	19.4	20.3	17.7	max	15.9	18.9	17.4
Switzerland	max	max	max	41.7	13.4	20.2	32.1	11.4	14.5	23.6	17.2	18.9	17.0	max	15.2	19.0	17.1
Austria	max	13.5	max	35.9	14.3	19.5	27.5	12.3	14.6	21.7	18.1	19.0	20.9	max	18.1	19.7	18.9
Spain	max	max	32.1	max	18.5	24.5	max	16.8	19.5	27.2	20.1	21.9	23.9	max	21.5	28.1	24.8
Norway	max	max	max	max	max	max	max	max	max	27.2	28.5	28.1	26.3	max	max	29.6	26.0
Denmark	max	max	max	max	max	max	max	max	max	26.0	max	28.4	24.1	max	20.6	max	27.9
Mexico	max	max	max	41.7	max	29.1	33.6	23.8	30.0	max	28.4	27.5	26.3	max	max	34.4	28.4
Finland	max	max	max	max	max	max	33.6	max	max	25.3	max	max	21.0	max	18.1	26.9	22.5
Columbia	max	max	max	max	max	max	33.8	max	max	max	max	max	max	max	max	32.1	27.2
Israel	max	max	max	max	max	max	max	max	max	max	max	max	max	max	max	max	max
Portugal	max	max	max	max	max	max	33.8	23.8	max	25.8	28.1	27.5	23.9	max	20.5	31.3	25.9
Brazil*	max	max	max	41.9	max	29.2	33.8	23.8	25.3	26.5	21.5	27.4	23.1	max	19.4	19.2	19.3
Argentina*	max	max	max	max	max	max	max	max	max	27.3	27.6	27.4	25.7	max	21.9	26.7	24.3
India*	max	max	max	max	max	max	max	max	max	max	max	max	26.1	max	22.1	max	28.7
South Africa*	max	max	max	max	max	max	max	max	max	max	max	max	max	max	max	max	max
Chile*	max	max	max	max	max	max	max	max	max	max	max	max	max	max	max	32.7	27.5
Venezuela*	max	max	max	max	max	max	max	max	max	max	max	max	max	max	max	max	max
Turkey*	max	max	max	max	max	max	max	max	max	max	max	max	max	max	max	26.8	24.6

(continued)

Table C–5 *(continued)*

	1952 Plastics	1952 Synthetic Rubbers	1952 Plastics & Rubbers	1952 Man-made Fibres	1952 Total Synthetics	1957 Plastics	1957 Synthetic Rubbers	1957 Plastics & Rubbers	1957 Man-made Fibres	1957 Total Synthetics	1962 Plastics	1962 Synthetic Rubbers	1962 Plastics & Rubbers	1962 Man-made Fibres	1962 Total Synthetics
MAXIMUM LAG	25·9	13·7	22·0	35·4	27·5	27·1	17·5	24·1	37·8	27·9	29·6	22·0	27·6	40·2	30·4
United States	2·8	0·6	2·0	7·7	4·4	2·9	0·4	2·1	7·2	3·5	2·5	0·6	2·0	6·9	3·1
Germany	1·8	11·7	5·2	1·0	3·5	2·7	12·7	5·9	1·5	4·6	2·5	13·2	5·4	2·2	4·7
United Kingdom	8·5	max	10·2	6·1	8·5	7·4	17·4	10·6	6·4	9·4	8·1	18·1	10·8	6·6	9·8
France	9·1	max	10·7	9·7	10·3	10·5	16·7	12·5	9·8	11·7	10·7	17·1	12·4	10·2	11·8
Italy	16·3	max	15·4	13·9	14·8	14·9	max	15·8	13·1	15·1	14·4	18·2	15·4	12·5	14·7
Japan	12·9	max	13·1	15·3	14·0	13·5	max	14·7	14·6	14·6	13·2	20·2	15·1	14·1	14·8
Canada	15·0	6·2	12·0	23·0	16·4	14·7	5·3	11·7	22·3	14·6	13·9	6·5	12·0	22·0	14·3
Netherlands	20·5	max	17·9	21·9	19·5	20·5	max	19·5	21·4	20·0	20·7	20·3	20·6	21·5	20·7
Sweden	20·3	max	17·9	23·0	19·8	19·4	max	18·8	23·1	20·0	19·5	21·7	20·1	24·2	21·1
Australia	20·4	max	17·9	max	24·9	20·0	max	19·2	37·2	24·2	19·5	21·3	20·0	39·1	24·4
Belgium	18·5	max	16·9	18·7	17·6	19·0	max	18·5	18·7	18·5	20·6	21·7	20·9	18·4	20·3
Switzerland	16·4	max	15·5	19·6	17·1	17·9	max	17·7	19·3	18·1	17·8	max	18·9	19·9	19·1
Austria	21·7	max	19·0	20·5	19·6	21·7	max	20·4	20·8	20·5	21·5	21·8	21·7	22·1	21·8
Spain	23·1	max	19·9	22·6	21·0	22·3	max	21·4	20·0	21·0	22·4	max	22·2	22·4	22·3
Norway	24·9	max	21·1	29·5	24·9	24·0	max	21·9	30·1	24·2	24·5	max	23·8	26·8	24·5
Denmark	23·6	max	20·2	max	26·3	24·2	max	22·0	max	26·4	27·4	max	25·9	max	29·1
Mexico	25·1	max	21·2	34·0	26·3	23·6	max	21·7	32·4	24·7	23·2	max	22·9	30·9	24·7
Finland	21·6	max	18·9	25·9	21·7	22·6	max	21·0	24·8	22·1	24·8	max	24·1	31·8	24·3
Columbia	max	max	max	32·2	26·1	max	max	max	31·9	26·3	max	max	max	39·5	28·5
Israel	max	max	max	max	max	26·6	max	23·7	37·7	27·6	29·0	max	27·1	max	20·0
Portugal	24·2	max	20·6	32·1	25·2	25·5	max	23·0	32·8	25·7	28·0	max	26·4	33·0	27·9
Brazil*	22·1	max	19·2	19·8	19·4	21·9	max	20·5	19·6	20·3	21·3	max	21·4	19·6	20·9
Argentina*	24·8	max	21·0	25·9	23·0	25·2	max	22·8	25·3	23·5	26·0	max	24·9	24·9	24·9
India*	25·3	max	21·3	35·1	26·8	25·8	max	23·2	35·0	26·5	26·9	max	25·6	34·3	27·6
South Africa*	max	max	max	max	max	26·7	max	23·8	max	27·7	28·0	max	26·4	max	29·5
Chile*	max	max	max	33·2	26·5	26·9	max	23·9	35·0	27·0	29·1	max	27·2	35·6	29·1
Venezuela*	max	max	max	26·0	23·6	max	max	max	37·4	27·8	max	max	max	39·0	30·2
Turkey*	max	max	max	max	max	max	max	max	25·6	24·5	max	max	max	25·8	27·1

Table C–6.   Approximate Annual Wage Rates in the Chemical Industry

Current $ at Current Exchange Rates

	1952	1957	1962
United States	3850	4080	4860
Germany	960	1150	1800
United Kingdom	1140	1480	2270
France	900	1000	1550
Italy	630	850	1060
Japan	520	610	1020
Canada	3120	3180	4190
Netherlands	710	1000	1420
Sweden	1500	2410	3060
Australia	1650	1760	2080
Belgium	1100	1380	1650
Switzerland	1700	1830	2150
Austria	680	840	1150
Spain	220	260	350
Norway	1330	1940	2520
Denmark	1230	1750	2280
Mexico	580	610	900
Finland	1200	1430	1920
Columbia	300	400	450
Israel	660	1010	1230
Portugal	220	260	350

Source: International Labour Organisation, *Yearbook of Labour Statistics*, and estimates therefrom.

Table C–7.   Approximate Gross Domestic Products

Billions of $U.S. at 1955 Prices

	1913	1920	1930	1940	1950	1960
United States	97·0	125·0	168·3	198·0	294·0	409·0
Germany*	37·5	38·7	41·2	43·2	31·8	70·6
United Kingdom	42·0	42·0	43·0	50·9	54·7	73·0
France	16·0	19·7	24·7	24·5	32·4	53·5
Italy	8·0	9·3	11·1	12·5	16·7	30·8
Japan	4·8	6·7	9·5	12·3	11·1	27·7
Canada	7·2	8·5	10·3	12·2	20·0	29·2
Netherlands	3·1	3·6	4·5	5·7	7·6	12·2
Sweden	2·4	3·1	4·2	5·9	8·3	12·8
Australia	4·5	5·6	7·1	8·5	12·3	16·5
Belgium	5·8	5·9	6·2	7·5	10·3	14·1
Switzerland	1·9	2·3	2·9	3·4	4·8	8·2
Austria	2·3	2·4	2·6	2·6	3·1	5·5
Spain	3·9	4·3	5·0	6·2	7·9	11·4
Norway	1·2	1·4	1·8	2·5	3·2	4·6
Denmark	1·7	2·1	2·6	3·3	4·1	6·4
Mexico	2·0	2·4	3·2	4·7	6·0	9·2
Finland	1·0	1·1	1·2	1·7	2·2	3·6
Colombia	1·0	1·1	1·2	1·7	2·6	4·1
Israel	—	—	—	—	0·8	2·4
Portugal	1·2	1·3	1·5	1·9	2·4	3·5

* West Germany after 1945.
Sources: A. Maizels, *Industrial Growth and World Trade*, 1963; *International Financial Statistics;* United Nations, *Yearbook of National Accounts Statistics*.

Table C–8. Approximate Production of Plastics and Synthetic Rubbers

Thousand Metric Tons

	1910 Plastics	1920 Plastics	1930 Plastics	1940 Plastics	1940 Rubbers	1950 Plastics	1950 Rubbers	1960 Plastics	1960 Rubbers
United States	0·5	13·0	26·5	163·0	2·6	1030·0	476·0	2270·0	1436·0
Germany*	6·9	17·5	23·1	69·9	39·4	84·4	1·8	964·0	79·8
United Kingdom	0·3	2·0	10·2	42·7	—	158·0	—	570·0	90·4
France	4·6	4·9	8·5	11·2	—	33·4	—	347·0	17·2
Italy	—	—	1·3	11·6	—	22·8	—	297·0	66·0
Japan	—	2·7	5·6	27·0	—	58·0	—	635·0	18·8
Canada	—	—	—	1·7	—	33·2	58·4	136·0	160·0
Netherlands	—	—	—	—	—	11·4	—	76·0	12·0
Sweden	—	—	—	2·5	—	14·5	—	65·9	—
Australia	—	—	—	—	—	13·0	—	51·1	—
Belgium	—	—	—	1·0	—	5·0	—	39·5	—
Switzerland	—	—	—	—	—	5·0	—	32·0	—
Austria	—	—	—	—	—	0·8	—	36·5	—
Spain	—	—	—	1·3	—	—	—	40·4	—
Norway	—	—	—	—	—	0·9	—	27·8	—
Denmark	—	—	—	—	—	—	—	7·0	—

* West Germany after 1945.
Sources: Consult Table C–19.

Table C–9.   Approximate Production of Man-Made Fibres

Thousand Metric Tons

	1910	1920	1930	1940	1950	1960
United States	0·2	4·6	57·8	213·0	625·0	773·0
Germany*	1·4	1·8	29·3	319·0	163·0	299·0
United Kingdom	1·1	2·9	21·2	76·7	168·0	268·0
France	1·2	1·5	22·9	26·6	83·2	163·0
Italy	—	0·7	30·4	162·0	104·0	195·0
Japan	—	0·1	16·8	227·0	115·0	495·0
Canada	—	—	2·1	8·9	26·4	51·3
Netherlands	—	0·2	8·0	11·8	33·2	58·4
Sweden	—	—	0·2	3·6	13·7	28·0
Australia	—	—	—	—	—	9·7
Belgium	0·5	2·9	5·8	6·2	23·0	33·8
Switzerland	0·1	0·6	4·6	5·5	17·2	28·2
Austria	0·5	0·7	0·8	19·9	32·7	57·8
Spain	—	0·1	1·2	3·1	24·4	57·1
Norway	—	—	—	0·3	13·3	14·3
Denmark	—	—	—	—	—	0·1
Mexico	—	—	—	—	9·1	24·7
Finland	—	—	—	0·2	7·8	16·4
Columbia	—	—	—	0·3	1·7	7·9
Israel	—	—	—	—	—	0·3
Portugal	—	—	—	0·1	0·9	2·3

* West Germany after 1945.
Sources: Consult Table C–19.

Table C-10. Multiple Correlation Coefficients (R^2)

Lambda Values		LINEAR					SEMI-LOG					DOUBLE LOG					SEMI-LOG & DOUBLE LOG				
		0·50	0·75	0·90	0·95	1·00	0·50	0·75	0·90	0·95	1·00	0·50	0·75	0·90	0·95	1·00	0·50	0·75	0·90	0·95	1·00
PLASTICS & SYNTHETIC RUBBERS	1952	0·887	0·895	0·893	0·896	0·904	0·795	0·811	0·825	0·335	0·848	0·765	0·781	0·774	0·772	0·773	0·768	0·748	0·751	0·751	0·700
	1957	0·970	0·971	0·971	0·969	0·967	0·826	0·824	0·831	0·833	0·843	0·780	0·816	0·830	0·818	0·811	0·800	0·832	0·830	0·820	0·813
	1962	0·931	0·952	0·934	0·937	0·935	0·656	0·643	0·640	0·640	0·641	0·786	0·748	0·707	0·722	0·716	0·738	0·702	0·672	0·682	0·679
MAN-MADE FIBRES	1952	0·687	0·687	0·678	0·680	0·691	0·716	0·726	0·731	0·737	0·739	0·530	0·731	0·813	0·847	0·849	0·779	0·809	0·836	0·850	0·853
	1957	0·841	0·849	0·728	0·782	0·799	0·784	0·784	0·782	0·781	0·779	0·598	0·691	0·812	0·846	0·851	0·808	0·809	0·824	0·835	0·842
	1962	0·874	0·866	0·901	0·931	0·907	0·841	0·840	0·838	0·834	0·836	0·736	0·866	0·933	0·932	0·915	0·888	0·920	0·927	0·917	0·907
AVERAGE		0·832	0·852	0·851	0·866	0·867	0·770	0·771	0·775	0·778	0·781	0·699	0·772	0·812	0·823	0·819	0·797	0·803	0·807	0·809	0·807

Table C–11. Parameter Values

		Lag (a)	Wages (b)	Income (c)	Production (d)
PLASTICS &	1952	−2·613	0·719	0·535	−0·170
SYNTHETIC	1957	−1·441	0·465	0·483	0·037
RUBBERS	1962	−1·261	0·020	0·207	0·077
MAN-MADE	1952	−2·216	−0·045	0·040	−0·111
FIBRES	1957	−0·992	0·200	−0·345	0·323
	1962	−0·634	−0·207	−0·358	0·374

Table C–12. Revised Parameter Values; 70% Confidence Ranges (in parentheses)

		Lag (a)	Wages (b)	Income (c)	Production (d)
	1952	−1·527 (±0·589)		0·531* (±0·317)	
PLASTICS & SYNTHETIC RUBBERS	1957	−1·600 (±0·307)		0·635 (±0·054)	
	1962	−1·269 (±0·246)		0·215 (±0·050)	0·076 (±0·017)
	1952	−1·895 (±0·256)	−0·108 (±0·171)		
MAN-MADE FIBRES	1957	−1·441 (±0·347)	−0·112 (±0.250)		0·098* (±0·051)
	1962	−1·270 (±0·233)	−0·413 (±0·189)		0·137 (±0·031)

* Asterisked values are not significant at the 95% confidence level.

Table C–13. Final Parameter Values; 70% Confidence Ranges (in parentheses); Partial Correlation Coefficients (*underlined*); Multiple Correlation Coefficients (R)

		Lag (a)	Wages (b)	Income (c)	Production (d)	Multiple Correlation Coefficient (R)
PLASTICS & SYNTHETIC RUBBERS	1952	−1·527		0·531*		0. 905
		(±0·589)		(±0·317)		
		−0·455		0·722		
	1957	−1·600		0·635		0·977
		(±0·307)		(±0·054)		
		−0·700		0·911		
	1962	−1·269		0·215	0·076	0·965
		(±0·246)		0·050	(±0·017)	
		−0·647		0·345	0·278	
MAN-MADE FIBRES	1952	−1·861				0·820
		(±0·259)				
		−0·820				
	1957	−1·552			0·075*	0·809
		(±0·357)			(±0·049)	
		−0·575			0·216	
	1962	−1·270	−0·413		0·137	0·919
		(±0·233)	(±0·189)		(±0·031)	
		−0·697	−0·427		0·525	

* Asterisked values are not significant at the 95% confidence level.

Table C–14. Past Production Related to Past Lags, Past Income

	Partial Correlation Coefficients		
	1961 $\sum$ L 1910	1961 $\sum$ Y 1913	Multiple Correlation Coefficient (R)
Plastics & Rubbers 1962	−0·542	0·901	0·965
Man-Made Fibres 1962	−0·892	0·950	0·980

Table C–15. Simple Correlation Coefficients between Independent Variables

		Lag (a)	Wages (b)	Income (c)	Production (d)
	1952				
	Income	−0·729			
PLASTICS &	1957				
SYNTHETIC	Income	−0·755			
RUBBERS	1962				
	Income	−0·744			0·947
	Production	−0·835		0·947	
	1957				
	Production	−0·767			
MAN-MADE	1962				
FIBRES	Wages	−0·239			0·431
	Production	−0·771	0·431		

Note: Correlation coefficients are only given for the parameters which appear in Table C–13.

Table C–16. Parameter Values for Difference Equations

		Lag ($\dot{a}$)	Wages ($\dot{b}$)	Income ($\dot{c}$)	Production ($\dot{d}$)
PLASTICS &	1957-1952	4·30	1·40	3·18	0·79
SYNTHETIC					
RUBBERS	1962-1957	−2·44	0·51	1·23	−0·59
MAN-MADE	1957-1952	1·98	−0·52	4·61	1·02
FIBRES	1962-1957	0·94	1·45	−0·74	0·38

Table C-17. Revised Parameter Values for Difference Equations; 70% Confidence Ranges (in parentheses)

		Lag (â)	Wages (b̂)	Income (ċ)	Production (d̂)
PLASTICS & SYNTHETIC	1957-1952			3·76 (±1·02)	0·70 (±0·15)
RUBBERS	1962-1957	−1·66 (±1·79)		3·24 (±0·59)	
MAN-MADE FIBRES	1957-1952		−0·37 (±0·69)	4·52 (±1·06)	1·05 (±0·34)
	1962-1957				0·48* (±0·29)

* Not significant at the 95% confidence level.

Table C-18. Final Parameter Values for Difference Equations; 70% Confidence Ranges (in parentheses); Partial Correlation Coefficients (*underlined*); Multiple Correlation Coefficients (R)

		Lag (â)	Wages (b̂)	Income (ċ)	Production (d̂)	Multiple Correlation Coefficient (R)
PLASTICS & SYNTHETIC RUBBERS	1957-1952			3·76 (±1·02) 0·532	0·70 (±0·15) 0·699	0·634
	1962-1957			3·20 (±0·57) 0·782		0·782
MAN-MADE FIBRES	1957-1952			4·38 (±0·94) 0·661	1·10 (±0·30) 0·572	0·675
	1962-1957				0·48* (±0·29) 0·377	0·377

* Not significant at the 95% confidence level.

Table C–19. World Production and Exports (Metric Tons)

Year	Plastics Production	Plastics Exports	Synthetic Rubbers Production	Synthetic Rubbers Exports	Man-Made Fibres Production	Man-Made Fibres Exports
1900	10,000	na	—	—	1,000	na
1905	na	na	—	—	4,000	na
1910	13,000	na	—	—	5,500	na
1911	na	na	—	—	7,300	na
1912	na	na	—	—	8,600	na
1913	35,000	3,000	—	—	11,000	na
1914	na	na	—	—	9,500	na
1915	na	na	—	—	6,800	na
1916	na	na	200	—	9,500	na
1917	na	na	1,000	—	10,000	na
1918	na	na	1,000	—	11,000	na
1919	na	na	—	—	13,000	na
1920	na	na	—	—	15,000	4,800
1921	na	na	—	—	22,000	6,800
1922	na	na	—	—	35,000	7,100
1923	na	na	—	—	46,000	12,000
1924	50,000	5,000	—	—	64,000	16,000
1925	na	na	—	—	83,000	23,000
1926	na	na	—	—	95,000	27,000
1927	na	na	—	—	130,000	42,000
1928	na	na	—	—	158,000	46,000
1929	na	na	—	—	196,000	53,000
1930	75,000	10,000	—	—	202,000	55,000
1931	na	na	—	—	220,000	56,000
1932	80,000	na	—	—	236,000	49,000
1933	na	na	—	—	302,000	52,000
1934	na	na	—	—	360,000	66,000
1935	150,000	na	—	—	474,000	62,000
1936	na	na	—	—	583,000	90,000
1937	170,000	15,000	3,100	—	814,000	121,000
1938	300,000	33,000	6,100	—	868,000	94,000
1939			24,000	—	1,000,000	na
1940	na	na	42,000	—	1,100,000	na
1941	na	na	77,000	na	1,250,000	na
1942	na	na	121,000	na	1,190,000	na
1943	na	na	350,000	na	1,150,000	na
1944	600,000	na	901,000	na	911,000	na
1945	500,000	na	866,000	na	605,000	na
1946	na	na	809,000	86,000	755,000	66,000
1947	870,000	60,000	568,000	27,000	904,000	93,000
1948	950,000	na	541,000	27,000	1,090,000	118,000
1949	1,050,000	na	447,000	38,000	1,170,000	127,000
1950	1,500,000	150,000	543,000	47,000	1,150,000	198,000

(continued)

Table C–19.   World Production and Exports
(continued)

Year	Plastics		Synthetic Rubbers		Man-Made Fibres	
	Production	Exports	Production	Exports	Production	Exports
1951	1,800,000	210,000	923,000	45,000	1,730,000	250,000
1952	1,800,000	170,000	892,000	88,000	1,510,000	179,000
1953	2,100,000	230,000	951,000	69,000	1,780,000	235,000
1954	2,400,000	340,000	727,000	94,000	1,930,000	268,000
1955	3,000,000	450,000	1,003,000	165,000	2,200,000	336,000
1956	3,400,000	540,000	1,230,000	236,000	2,320,000	360,000
1957	3,800,000	660,000	1,283,000	305,000	2,480,000	377,000
1958	4,200,000	800,000	1,263,000	307,000	2,250,000	378,000
1959	5,200,000	1,020,000	1,665,000	421,000	2,620,000	464,000
1960	5,700,000	1,100,000	1,895,000	553,000	2,780,000	509,000
1961	7,000,000	1,375,000	2,025,000	545,000	2,930,000	526,000
1962	7,950,000	1,650,000	2,280,000	593,000	3,330,000	656,000

(na) not available. (—) negligible.
Production and exports by countries now members of the Communist block are excluded throughout the table. Figures for early years are mainly guesses.

Sources:
Plastics—J. Delorme, *Le Commerce des Matières Plastiques dans le Monde*, 1956; J. Delorme, *Le Présent et L'Avenir des Matières Plastiques*, 1954; E. B. von Wehrenalp and H. Saechtling, *Jarhundert der Kunststoff in Wort und Bild*, 1952; *Industrial Chemist*; *Plastics Technology*; *Plastiques Informations*; OECD, *The Chemical Industry in Europe*; OECD, *Industrial Statistics 1900–1959*, 1960; U.S. Department of Commerce, *World Survey of Plastics 1954–1957*, 1959; U.S. Tariff Commission, *Synthetic Resins and their Raw Materials*, 1938; official trade and production statistics.
Synthetic Rubbers—*Rubber Statistical Bulletin*; G. S. Whitby, *Synthetic Rubbers*, 1954; official trade and production statistics.
Man-Made Fibres—*Artificial Silk World*; *Rayon Record*; *Silk and Rayon*; *Textile Organon*; OECD, *The Textile Industry in Europe*; official trade statistics.

Table C–20.   Recent High Pressure Polyethylene Plants

Country	Producer	Comple-tion Date	Capacity Metric Tons	Cost[a] $U.S. mill.
United States	Dow Chemical	1962	23,000	$ 6·0
United States	U.S. Industrial Chem.	1963	27,000	15·0
United States	Rexall Chemical	1962	55,000	20·0
United Kingdom	Bakelite-Xylonite	1960	25,000	12·6
Italy	Rumianca SPA	1964	10,000	9·0
Japan	Nippon Petrochemical	na	30,000	13·9
Japan	Mitsubishi Chemical	1965	20,000	11.1
Japan	Mitsui Chemical	1961	18,000	13·5
Japan	Nitto Chemical	1962	27,000	10·0
Canada	Canadian Indus. Chem.	1959	18,000	15·0
Sweden	Unifos Kemi	1963	15,000	7·7
Australia	ICIANZ	1957	10,000	7·3
Australia	Union Carbide Australia	1962	14,000	20·0
Australia	Hoechst	na	10,000	10·1
Spain	Alcudia	1965	30,000	56·0
Denmark	Danbritkam A/S	1962	15,000	11·2
Israel	Israeli Petrochemical	1963	6,000	15·1
Brazil	Union Carbide do Brazil	1962	11,000	12·5
Argentina	Ind. Quim. Arg. Duperial	1960	10,000	16·1
South Africa	African Expl. & Chem.	1965	28,000	16·8
Pakistan	Manzoor Chemicals	1965	5,000	9·8

(a) Converted at current exchange rates.
Source: Temple Press Intelligence Unit, *Plant Information Sheets*, 1964 and earlier years.

Table C–21. Recent Polypropylene Plants

Country	Producer	Completion Date	Capacity Metric Tons	Cost[a] $U.S. mill.
United States	Humble Chemicals	1961	45,000	$12·0
United States	Avi-Sun	1961	46,000	20·0
United Kingdom	I.C.I.	1961	11,000	8·4
Japan	Mitsui Chemical	1962	10,000	20·6
Japan	Chisso Petrochemical	1963	13,000	21·4
Japan	Yawata	1961	10,000	7·0
Japan	Mitsubishi	1962	10,000	9·0
Netherlands	N.V. Rotterdamse Polyolefinen	1963	10,000	20·0
Austria	Danubia Petrochemie AG	1962	5,000	9·6
India	West Polymer WKS	1965	7,000	31·0

(a) Converted at current exchange rates.
Source: Temple Press Intelligence Unit, *Plant Information Sheets*, 1964 and earlier years.

Table C-22. Recent Polyvinyl Chloride Plants

Country	Producer	Completion Dated	Capacity Metric Tons	Cost[a] $U.S. mill.
United States	Borden Chemical	na	18,000	$ 4·0
United States	Pentasote Co.	1961/62	20,000	1·7
United States	Cary Chemical	1962	40,000	4·0
United Kingdom	British Geon	1962	45,000	7·6
Italy	Rumianca SPA	1962	10,000	3·0
Japan	Japanese Geon	1964	16,800	1·7
Japan	Kanegafuchi	1964	16,800	4·3
Japan	Mitsubishi-Monsanto	1965	12,000	5·6
Australia	BF Goodrich	1962	7,000	3·5
Israel	Trutarom	1963	4,000	4·0
India	Dhrangadrs Chemical	na	12,000	11·9

(a) Converted at current exchange rates.
Sources: Temple Press Intelligence Unit, *Plant Information Sheets*, 1964 and earlier years; *Chemical Week*, September 2, 1961.

Table C-23. Recent Styrene Monomer Plants

Country	Producer	Completion Date	Capacity Metric Tons	Cost[a] $U.S. mill.
United States	Cosden-Grace	1957	32,000	$ 3·2
United States	Foster-Grant	1954	70,000	5·0
United States	Marbon Chemical	1963	35,000	5·0
United States	Monsanto Chemical	1962/63	250,000	30·0
United Kingdom	North Chemicals	1963	50,000	14·4
Japan	Osaka Gas	1965	18,000	2·8
Japan	Yawata	1961	15,000	4·2
Argentina	Argentina Koppers	1960	15,000	7·5
India	Hindustan Polymer	1963	10,000	10·5

(a) Converted at current exchange rates.
Sources: Temple Press Intelligence Unit, *Plant Information Sheets*, 1964 and earlier years; *Japan Chemical Week*, February 7, 1961.

BIBLIOGRAPHY

Academic Papers

K. J. Arrow, "The Economic Implications of Learning by Doing", *Review of Economic Studies*, July 1962.

K. J. Arrow, H. B. Chenery, B. S. Minhas, and R. M. Solow, "Capital-Labor Substitution and Economic Efficiency", *Review of Economics and Statistics*, August 1961.

R. E. Baldwin, "The Commodity Composition of Trade: Selected Industrial Countries, 1900–1954", *Review of Economics and Statistics*, February 1958.

D. M. Bensusan-Butt, "A Model of Trade and Accumulation", *American Economic Review*, September 1954.

A. K. Cairncross, "World Trade in Manufactures Since 1900", *Economia Internazionale*, November 1955.

A. K. Cairncross, J. Faaland, "Long-Term Trends in Europe's Trade", *Economic Journal*, March 1952.

C. H. Chilton, "Six-Tenths Factor Applies to Complete Plant Costs", *Chemical Engineering*, April 1950.

M. Chon, "Patterns of Industrial Growth", 1960 (Stanford Project).

G. K. Douglass, Pomona College, "Innovation and International Trade", unpublished as of January 1966.

A. Egendorf, Jr., Harvard College, "The Pure Theory of International Trade", and "Analysis: Specific Application of Multiple Regression", both unpublished as of January 1966.

C. Freeman, "The Plastics Industry: A Comparative Study of Research and Innovation", *National Institute Economic Review*, November 1963.

R. F. Harrod, "Factor-Price Relations under Free Trade", *Economic Journal*, June 1958.

E. F. Heckscher, "The Effect of Foreign Trade on the Distribution of Income", reprinted in *Readings in The Theory of International Trade*, 1949.

J. R. Hicks, "An Inaugural Lecture", *Oxford Economic Papers*, June 1953.

S. Hirsch, "The United States Electronics Industry in International Trade", *National Institute Economic Review*, November 1965.

G. Holton, "Scientific Research and Scholarship", *Daedalus*, Spring 1962.

C. O. Hoyer, "Factors in the Location of the Plastics Industry", *Chemical Engineering Progress*, May 1949.

N. Kaldor, "Comment", *Review of Economic Studies*, July 1962.

N. Kaldor, J. A. Mirrlees, "A New Model of Economic Growth", *Review of Economic Studies*, July 1962.

I. B. Kravis, " 'Availability' and Other Influences on the Commodity Composition of Trade", *Journal of Political Economy*, April 1956.

F. G. Lamont, "Genesis of a Chemical Industry", *New Scientist*, February 14, 1963.

W. W. Leontief, "Factor Proportions and the Structure of American Trade", *Review of Economics and Statistics*, November 1956.

W. W. Leontief, "Domestic Production and Foreign Trade: the American Capital Position Re-examined", *Economia Internazionale*, February 1954.

W. A. Lewis, "World Production, Prices, and Trade, 1870–1960", *The Manchester School*, May 1952.

G. D. A. MacDougall, "British and American Exports: A Study Suggested by the Theory of Comparative Costs, Part I; Part II", *Economic Journal*, December 1951; September 1952.

R. L. Major, "World Trade in Manufactures", *National Institute Economic Review*, July 1960.

E. Mansfield, "Size of Firm, Market Structure, and Innovation", *Journal of Political Economy*, December 1963.

M. Michaely, "The Shares of Countries in World Trade", *Review of Economics and Statistics*, August 1960.

B. S. Minhas, "The Homohypallagic Production Function", *Journal of Political Economy*, April 1962.

F. T. Moore, "Economies of Scale: Some Statistical Evidence", *Quarterly Journal of Economics*, May 1959.

D. C. Paige, *et al.*, "Economic Growth: The Last Hundred Years", *National Institute Economic Review*, July 1961.

N. Platzer, "Organic Polyvinyl Ester Production in Germany", *Modern Plastics*, September 1950.

M. V. Posner, "International Trade and Technical Change," *Oxford Economic Papers*, October 1961.

R. Robinson, "Factor Proportions and Comparative Advantage, Part I; Part II", *Quarterly Journal of Economics*, May 1956; August 1956.

P. A. Samuelson, "International Trade and the Equalisation of Factor Prices", *Economic Journal*, June 1948.

P. A. Samuelson, "International Factor-Price Equalisation Once Again", *Economic Journal*, June 1949.

A. N. Shimmin, "The Economic Problems of the Rayon Industry", *Artificial Silk World*, June 28, 1929.

H. Tyszynski, "World Trade in Manufactured Commodities 1899–1950", *The Manchester School*, September 1951.

R. Vernon, "International Investment in the Trade Cycle", unpublished as of January 1966.

Technical Journals Consulted. The following technical journals were examined extensively. The nationality of each journal is given in parenthesis.

Artificial Silk World (continued as *Rayon Record*; British).
British Plastics (British).
Chemical Age (British).
Chemical Engineering (American).
Chemical Engineering Progress (American).
Chemische Industrie (German).
Chemistry in Canada (Canadian).
Chemische Industrie International (German).
Canadian Plastics (Canadian).
Chemical and Rubber Industry Report (American).
Chemical Week (American).
European Chemical News (British).
Industrial Chemist (British).
Industrial and Engineering Chemistry (American).
Industrial Research (American).
Japan Chemical Week (Japanese).
Modern Plastics (American).
Oil, Paint, and Drug Reporter (American).
Plastvarlden (Swedish).
Plastiques Informations (French).
Plastics Materials Industry Report (American).
Plastics Technology (American).
Revue des Produits Chimiques (French).
Rayon Record (continuation of *Artificial Silk World*; continued as *Silk & Rayon*; British).
Rubber Statistical Bulletin (British).
Silk & Rayon (continuation of *Rayon Record*; continued as *Skinner's Silk & Rayon Record*; British).
Skinner's Silk & Rayon Record (continuation of *Silk & Rayon*; British).
Textile Organon (American).
Western Plastics (American).
World Petroleum (American).

Official Publications. In addition to the following publications, official trade statistics have been widely consulted.

Australian Department of Trade, *Plastics Industry of Australia*, 1958.
Dominion Bureau of Statistics (Canada), *Census of Production*, 1959 and earlier years.
Food and Agricultural Organisation, *Yearbook of Agricultural Statistics*, 1952.
Industrial Business Association of Japan, *Import of Techniques and Development of Industries*, 1961.

International Labour Organisation. *Yearbook of Labour Statistics*, 1963 and earlier years.

International Monetary Fund, *International Financial Statistics*, 1963 and earlier years.

League of Nations, Economic, Financial and Transit Department, *Industrialization and Foreign Trade*, 1945.

Ministry of International Trade and Industry (Japan), *Census of Production*, 1958 and earlier years.

Organisation for European Economic Cooperation, *The Chemical Industry In Europe*, 1961–62 and earlier years.

Organisation for European Economic Cooperation, *Comparative National Products and Price Levels* (by M. Gilbert and associates), 1958.

Organisation for European Economic Cooperation, *Industrial Statistics 1900–1959*, 1960.

Organisation for European Economic Cooperation, *The Textile Industry in Europe*, 1960–61 and earlier years.

U.K. Board of Trade, *Census of Production*, 1958 and earlier years.

U.K. Department of Scientific and Industrial Research, *Expenditure on Scientific Research and Technical Development in Britain and America*, 1956.

United Nations, *Commodity Trade Statistics*, 1955.

United Nations, *Statistical Yearbook*, 1963 and earlier years.

United Nations, *National Income and Its Distribution in Under-Developed Countries*, 1951.

U.S. Bureau of the Census, *Annual Survey of Manufactures*, 1962 and earlier years.

U.S. Bureau of the Census, *Census of Manufactures*, 1958 and earlier years.

U.S. Department of Commerce, *Business Statistics*, 1963 and earlier editions.

U.S. Department of Commerce, *Plastics in Germany 1939–1946*, 1946.

U.S. Department of Commerce, *Statistical Abstract of the United States*, 1962 and earlier years.

U.S. Department of Commerce, *World Survey of Plastics, 1954–1957*, 1959.

U.S. Federal Trade Commission, *Rates of Return for Identical Companies, 1940, 1947–1960*, 1962.

U.S. Tariff Commission, *Synthetic Organic Chemicals*, 1963 and earlier years.

U.S. Tariff Commission, *Synthetic Resins and their Raw Materials*, 1938.

U.S. vs. Du Pont, *118 Federal Supplement 41*, 1954.

Other Books.

J. Airov, *The Location of the Synthetic Fiber Industry*, 1959.

American Viscose Corporation, *50 Avisco Years*, 1960.

R. S. Aries, R. D. Newton, *Chemical Engineering Cost Estimation*, 1950.

G. S. Armstrong & Co., *An Engineering Interpretation of the Economic and Financial Aspects of American Industry*, 1940.

J. C. Avenarius, J. G. Keppler, *Plastics Veroveren de Wereld*, 1950.

P. G. Black, *Molded Plastics Products*, 1954.

J. F. Blais, *Amino Resins*, 1959.

W. N. Bowie, *et al.*, *Epoxy Resins: Market Survey and Users' Reference*, 1959.

A. J. Brown, *Industrialization and Trade: The Changing World Pattern and the Position of Britain*, 1943.

S. Burenstam-Linder, *An Essay on Trade and Transformation*, 1961.

C. Z. Carroll-Porczynski, *Inorganic Fibres*, 1958.

C. Z. Carroll-Porczynski, *Manual of Man-Made Fibres*, 1960.

E. R. Corey, *The Development of Markets for New Materials*, 1956.

D. B. Creamer, *et al.*, *Capital in Manufacturing and Mining* (National Bureau of Economic Research Study) 1960.

J. M. DeBell, *et al.*, *German Plastics Practice*, 1946.

J. Delorme, *Evolution et Rôle des Matières Plastiques Pendant la Guerre*, 1946.

J. Delorme, *Le Commerce des Matières Plastiques dans le Monde*, 1956.

J. Delorme, *Le Présent et l'Avenir des Matières Plastiques*, 1944.

J. Delorme, *Toute l'Industrie des Matières Plastiques*, 1936.

B. A. Dombrow, *Polyurethanes*, 1957.

A. G. Donnithorne, *British Rubber Manufacturing*, 1958.

J. H. DuBois, *Plastics*, 1943.

E. I. du Pont de Nemours & Co., *Annual Report*, 1960 and earlier years.

E. I. du Pont de Nemours & Co., *Du Pont Facts Book*.

Encyclopedia of Chemical Technology, 1957 and supplements.

T. J. Fielding, *History of Bakelite Ltd.*, 1948.

First National Bank of Boston, *The Plastics Industry in New England*, 1949.

D. E. Floyd, *Polyamide Resins*, 1958.

M. Fournier, *L'ère des Matières Plastiques*, 1951.

F. U. Gass, *Cellophan: Erfindung und Welterfolg*, 1956.

F. A. Graybill, *An Introduction to Linear Statistical Models*, Volume I, 1961.

L. F. Haber, *The Chemical Industry During the Nineteenth Century*, 1958.

G. Haberler, *A Survey of International Trade Theory*, 1955.

D. C. Hague, *The Economics of Man-Made Fibres*, 1957.

A. H. Hard, *The Rayon Year Book*, 1948.

A. H. Hard, *The Romance of Rayon*, 1933.

S. E. Harris, *International and Interregional Economics*, 1957.

W. Haynes, *American Chemical Industry: A History*, Volumes I–V, 1954–1958.

S. Hirsch, *Location of Industry and International Competitiveness* (unpublished D.B.A. dissertation), 1965.

A. O. Hirschman, *The Strategy of Economic Development*, 1958.

E. Hoffmeyer, *Dollar Shortage*, 1958.
M. B. Horn, *Acrylic Resins*, 1960.
V. Hottenroth, *Artificial Silk*, 1928.
G. C. Hufbauer, *Synthetic Materials: A Study in International Trade* (unpublished Ph.D. dissertation), 1963, Cambridge University Library.
D. W. Huke, *Introduction to Natural and Synthetic Rubbers*, 1961.
W. Isard, *et al.*, *Industrial Complex Analysis and Regional Development*, 1959.
Japan Daily Industry News, *Plastic Materials* (series), 1961.
Japan Fiber Association, *History of Japanese Fiber Industry*, 1958.
A. D. II. Kaplan, *et al.*, *Pricing in Big Business*, 1958.
C. P. Kindleberger, *Foreign Trade and the National Economy*, 1962.
C. P. Kindleberger, *International Economics*, 1963.
G. M. Kline, *The History and Uses of Plastics*, 1940.
A. P. Koch, *Die Deutsche Kunstwerkstoffindustrie*, 1939.
P. A. Koch, *Faserstoff Tabellen*, 1954 through 1962.
T. O. J. Kresser, *Polyethylene*, 1957.
T. O. J. Kresser, *Polypropylene*, 1960.
S. S. Kuznets, *National Income and its Composition, 1919–1938*, 1941.
J. R. Lawrence, *Polyester Resins*, 1960.
A. Maizels, *Industrial Growth and World Trade*, 1963.
J. Markham, *Competition in the Rayon Industry*, 1952.
Masselon, Roberts, and Cillard, *Celluloid; Its Manufacture, Applications, and Substitutes*, 1912.
H. R. Mauersberger, editor, *Matthew's Textile Fibers*, 1954.
R. R. McGregor, *Silicones and their Uses*, 1954.
J. E. Meade, *The Balance of Payments*, 1951.
J. E. Meade, *Trade and Welfare*, 1955.
R. N. Meals, F. M. Lewis, *Silicones*, 1959.
The Mercantile Marine Atlas, 1959.
R. W. Moncrieff, *Man-Made Fibres*, 1957.
S. Mookerjee, *Factor Endowments and International Trade*, 1958.
B. Ohlin, *Interregional and International Trade*, 1933.
Oil, Paint, and Drug Reporter, Hi-Lo Chemical Price Issue, 1962.
W. D. Paist, *Cellulosics*, 1958.
C. Piest, *Das Zelluloid*, 1913.
R. Rabald, *Die Absatzentwicklung auf dem Deutschen Rohcelluloidmark* (unpublished Ph.D. dissertation), 1951.
W. B. Reddaway, "The Chemical Industry", Chapter VI in D. L. Burn, editor, *Structure of British Industry*, 1958, volume I.
C. A. Redfarn, *A Guide to Plastics*, 1958.
F. Reinthaler, *Artificial Silk*, 1928.
A. Renfrew, P. Morgan, *Polythene*, 1960.
R. Robson, *The Man-Made Fibres Industry*, 1958.
L. Rostas, *Comparative Productivity in British and American Industry*, 1948.

M. A. Rudner, *Fluorocarbons*, 1958.

H. Saechtling, *Werkstoffe aus Menschenhand*, 1961.

W. E. G. Salter, *Productivity and Technical Change*, 1960.

P. A. Samuelson, *Principles of Economics*, 1961.

P. Schidrowitz, T. R. Dawson, *History of the Rubber Industry*, 1952.

J. A. Schumpeter, *Capitalism, Socialism, and Democracy*, 1950 (3rd edition).

I. Skeist, *Epoxy Resins*, 1958.

W. M. Smith, *Vinyl Resins*, 1958.

Society of the Plastics Industry, *Plastics*, 1961 and earlier editions.

H. J. Stern, *Rubber: Natural and Synthetic*, 1954.

E. Sutermeister, F. L. Browne, *Casein and its Industrial Applications*, 1939.

P. Sylos Labini, *Oligopoly and Technical Progress*, 1962.

W. C. Teach, G. C. Kiessling, *Polystyrene*, 1960.

Temple Press Intelligence Unit, *Plant Information Sheets* (plastics), 1963 and 1964.

M. S. Thompson, *Gum Plastics*, 1958.

Universities—National Bureau Committee for Economic Research, *The Rate and Direction of Inventive Activity*, 1962.

H. Voelcker, *75 Jahre Kalle*, 1948.

E. B. von Wehrenalp, H. Saechtling, *Jahrhundert der Kunststoff in Wort und Bild*, 1952.

G. S. Whitby, editor, *Synthetic Rubber*, 1954.

K. Winter, *Produktion und Standorte der Deutschen Kunstharzpressstoffindustrie*, 1938.

E. C. Worden, *Nitrocellulose Industry*, 1911.

AUTHOR INDEX

Footnote references are indicated by the letter *n* after the page number.

SUBJECT INDEX

Footnote references are indicated by the letter *n* after the page number. This index does not include subjects brought up in tables or diagrams.